The Mindful Breastfeeding Book

Preparing you for calm & connected feeding

Anna Le Grange

Illustrated by Jemma McCardle

This book is not intended as a substitute for medical advice.
The reader should regularly consult a doctor in matters relating to
their health or the health of their baby and particularly with respect
to any symptoms that may require diagnosis or medical attention.

For Noah, Elijah and Amélie

For teaching me more every day

and for being my reason why

Contents

Hello

Welcome to *The Mindful Breastfeeding Book*. Thank you so much for picking it up. I wrote it for expectant and brand new parents as a bit of a companion and an interactive guide to feeding your baby. Thinking and communicating about how we feed babies is such an important topic and one that has become very close to my heart. What I've discovered over more than 2 decades of supporting new parents, is that feeding babies comes with a whole host of feelings and emotions. From gut instincts to guilt, from joy to pain – as parents we feel a vast range of feelings from minute to minute and day to day.

This book addresses these emotions in a simple and practical way and I hope will support you in the same way that I do in my daily work as a Lactation Consultant – that is by looking at not only the practical side of breastfeeding but also the emotional one.

Mindfulness

Mindfulness has become a bit of a buzz word these days, a trend, and for some perhaps another thing to add to the ever expanding to-do list. So why are we all jumping on the mindfulness bandwagon? Well, if you're already on it then you will have your own reasons, but for me it's an antidote to my life and my busy personality. Both of which I love sincerely and would not be without. But my enthusiasm for most things and my tendency to take on too much, means that as a parent I can easily burn out, get stressed and overwhelmed.

I've enjoyed yoga since my early twenties but didn't prioritise it, putting work and socialising before rest and relaxation. As I became a parent and continued to work, I pushed time for myself further and further away. The mental to-do lists grew longer and more complicated. From juggling babies and toddlers with work to school runs, clubs and a new business. There seemed little time for anything more and I was doing everything for everybody except myself.

I had yearned for parenthood for so long. And I loved it. I loved the busyness of it and to some extent the juggling too. As a family we lived for our weekends and holidays. And life was good. But I found myself feeling guilty for not spending as much time with the children as I really should. I spent my time worrying about how that affected them and feeling guilty about not being the sort of parent that I should be to them. Despite working part time, I still felt that we were in a rat race. That life was always busy and we gave little time to just being. In many ways I was craving a simpler life.

The overwhelm, fear and guilt didn't take over my life, but it was always there in the background. It came out in arguments with my husband, in losing my temper with the children, in rushing them from one thing to another and in all honesty, being quite unhappy a lot of the time.

I decided that something had to give. I wanted to work in a more flexible way and I wanted to follow my passion of supporting families with breastfeeding. I spent a couple of years training, whilst continuing to volunteer and work. The hard work paid off because I did end up with a job that meant I could be with my children more. A job that didn't require as much childcare and a job that I truly loved.

Working with families who were at the very beginning of their parenting journey, I began to notice some of the familiar patterns starting to form for them too. For many families, having a baby in the first place had become a time-consuming, stressful and over-whelming thing. Pregnancy, full of worry and fear about doing the right thing. And then once the baby has arrived, these emotions becoming more amplified. I see anxiety and fear in almost every family I work with, and I see many parents, right at the start, already feeling overwhelmed by the intensity of parenthood.

And parenthood is overwhelming! Those little beings need EVERYTHING from us. But that in itself is not the only pressure we have. We come into parenthood with so many pre-constructed ideas of what parenting should be. Before our baby arrives, we have an image of parenthood, that almost certainly will be different to the reality. We also have expectations from our family and friends. Society puts a huge number of expectations on us as parents and this filters through to us from the media and from books and magazines that we read. It comes from our friends who are already parents and want to give us advice. And we lap it up for the most part because, initially, it helps to allay those fears that we're going to do everything wrong.

Bit by bit I started putting Mindfulness into my life as a parent and it turned things around, almost overnight. It made me happier, more relaxed and more in-the-moment with my children. It helped me to communicate more effectively with my husband and see what was important and what wasn't important in my life. It helped me to follow my instincts as a parent and shut out the "shoulds" coming from elsewhere.

Mindful Breastfeeding was born

I started to add Mindfulness techniques into the support I provided to breastfeeding families. I didn't want them to be 10 years into parenting before they recognised the stress they were under. I wanted to give them the tools right at the beginning of their parenting journey. Just like I wish someone had done for me.

What I discovered is that when parents have Mindfulness tools and a deep understanding of how important self-care is, that breastfeeding becomes a whole lot less overwhelming. That they are able to connect with and understand their baby in a deeper way. That they start to parent in THEIR way, not somebody else's. That they are able to navigate their own learning and trust that it leads to a happier breastfeeding relationship.

This was a revelation to me. That something psychological could have such a deep impact on something that we think of as a practical task. As soon as I saw how affective the techniques were I decided to share them with as many families, healthcare professionals and breastfeeding supporters as possible.

This book will support you as you prepare to feed your baby and it will provide you with the information you need to get breastfeeding off to a good start. It's full of pictures, practical know-how and exercises to help you uncover how you actually feel about feeding your baby.

Each chapter has journaling questions at the end which will give you insight, clarity and confidence as you transition into this next phase of your life as a parent.

You can work through the book alone or with your partner. The guided relaxations that are included with the book can be downloaded online. Go to:

http://mindfulbreastfeeding.co.uk/book-resources/

Sometimes, exploring our feelings and emotions can bring up past experiences and events and highlight issues that we may have been having for some time, but hadn't recognised or been aware of. If this is something that you experience whist going through this book, then I recommend seeking some support. This may be in the form of a talking therapy. Seeing your GP is a good place to start. However I have listed below some UK based peri-natal mental health organisations and helplines that you may find useful.

Mind:
https://www.mind.org.uk/information-support/

Pandas Foundation:
http://www.pandasfoundation.org.uk/

Family Action:
https://www.family-action.org.uk/what-we-do/early-years/perinatal-support-services/

chapter one
UNDERSTANDING INFANT FEEDING

As we enter into parenthood, whether it be our first, second or sixth time, we come into it with a whole range of preconceptions, idea, fears and judgements about the life we are about to embark on. Whether it's the type of parents we want or don't want to be or about how babies should behave, sleep or feed, our subconscious has a picture of how we expect things to be.

Our subconscious brain is what lies underneath. It is

the non-thinking part of our brain, the part that holds memories and our automatic actions and responses. As we go through life we save or "download" images, ideas and experiences into our subconscious, where they sit, often quite deep down, and guide our feelings and actions. These experiences or "stories" can feel like our truth and who we think we are as a person. We see them as our beliefs and values but they can also be our fears and anxieties.

When it comes to our subconscious, we don't only build up pictures from the physical experiences that we've had, but also those that we have witnessed and heard from others, whether it be in real life or on the TV, internet or in books. If you think about it, there will be a whole host of things that you have opinions and feelings about even if you haven't experienced them yourself.

I, for example, have never climbed Mount Everest. I don't plan on doing this either and haven't spent any time researching how to do it. However, I have lots of ideas and images on what it might be like. I know that Everest is covered in snow and ice and that I would need specialist climbing equipment like ropes, a harness, carabiners and crampons. I would need thermal clothing and I would sleep in a tent during the journey. I would, most likely, have to train for months and that it's quite a trek to get to base camp alone. How do I know these things? I don't know anyone who has experienced an expedition like that, but since I first heard of Mount Everest my subconscious mind has been building up a picture of what it may be like. From photographs, Hollywood movies, magazine articles, news stories and conversations, my mind has been building up, layer upon layer, information about climbing Mount Everest so that I have quite an opinion on it and can, to some extent, imagine what it would be like.

When you break down your thought processes and memory like this it can be really mind blowing. The layers upon layers of experiences that we use just for everyday functions is immense. 40–95 per cent of the functions that we carry out are automatic, meaning that we have learned how to do them so well that we can now do them without consciously thinking. Consider opening a door, walking up-stairs, even driving at times, we are on autopilot for much of it.

So what may we have picked up about infant feeding throughout our lives? Trust me, there will be plenty that you haven't even considered.

How were you fed as a baby?

This is a great place to start as it helps us to think about the values and beliefs our family has about infant feeding. Perhaps you don't even know. If you are fortunate enough to have parents or family members around to ask about this, then do. It can open up conversations about all sorts of things. For example my mother started out breastfeeding me in hospital. Babies were put into a strict schedule of 4 hourly feeding in the hospital I was born at. My mother's supply started dipping and she was soon advised to top me up with formula after each breastfeed. After several exhausting weeks of doing this she decided that due to not having enough milk and feeding taking so long, it was better for us all to move me onto formula. A year later she had my brother and breastfed him for much longer. He was a much more demanding baby and at the new hospital where he had been born, they were encouraging mothers to take a more "feed-on-demand" view point. That, coupled with a baby who was often unsettled, meant that he was fed more frequently and therefore her milk supply kept going and she was able to breastfeed for a lot longer. My mum was always very positive about breastfeeding but had clearly found the experience of feeding me quite hard. It's something that now, even 40 years later, she still has feelings of sadness about.

What about other members of your family? Do you remember your siblings being fed? Perhaps nieces or nephews? Cousins? Family friends? If you were older, perhaps you remember having an opinion on this. Was it normal for you to see breastfeeding or did it make you feel uncomfortable? It can be useful to answer these questions with your partner. It's a really interesting conversation to have before your baby arrives. It will give you a sense of each other's view point before you head into this new chapter of your lives. If you are in the fortunate position of having your parents around, then having these conversations with them can be pure gold. They are likely to enjoy recounting your early days and it can also give a hint as to whether any of their own deep-seated beliefs around normal infant behavior may come up once your baby arrives. Again, knowing their own views and stories can be useful. It's likely to shape any comments or suggestions that they make to you about parenting. By understanding where these come from on an emotional and subconscious level, it can prevent us from taking any criticism too personally. It can also prepare you for what may come up and help you to understand why they are saying what they say. In quite a profound way, this frees you up to parent in your own way, right from the very start.

It can be very powerful to examine our thoughts and beliefs. When we look deeper into our own truth about breastfeeding and pick apart why we feel like we do, it opens us up and helps us recognise any conflicts that may have otherwise been hidden away. This clarity helps us to recognise any fear and anxieties that may come up and understand where they come from. The more we understand our fears the easier it is to find ways of releasing them.

JOURNALING PROMPTS

When working with families to help them unravel their truth around infant feeding, I always suggest writing things down. Journaling is a great tool for self-exploration and making sense of our feelings and emotions. Journaling can help us to access our deeper thoughts. You can use this space to write about your family experience of infant feeding in your life so far.

How subtle images of infant feeding infiltrate our subconscious

In the UK we live in a bottle-feeding culture and one which sexualises breasts. This has an absolutely huge impact on our feelings about breastfeeding, whether we realise it or not.

Let's start with the standard symbol for a baby – it's a bottle! When was the last time you heard of a toy doll that is marketed to feed at the breast? Most of them include bottles. You see, these messages and images start to penetrate our subconscious at a very young age. Ask a group of four year olds how babies are fed and what do you think the answer would be? It's virtually impossible to buy a toy doll that doesn't come with a bottle, so those subtle messages of bottle feeding have already started.

As the years go by we continue to build up this picture of infant feeding from the things we see. But what about the things we hear?

Have you ever heard any of the following things said? Perhaps you've said or thought them yourself. I know I did before I became a parent.

"I'm all for breastfeeding but it should be done in private."

"That baby is using her mum as a dummy."

"Why not express milk and feed with a bottle when out and about?"

Breastfeeding is fine until they have teeth / are walking / can ask for it."

"What about Dad? When does he get a look in?"

These statements demonstrate how we view breasts in our culture, primarily as sexual organs of a woman's body. They are thought of as private and for sexual enjoyment with our partners, rather than the part of the body that feeds a baby. Many men and women find breasts sexually attractive. So for some, when a baby is feeding at a breast and is latched onto and sucking on a nipple, it can bring up confusing feelings and emotions.

For a woman, if breasts have played a large part in her sex life, she may feel confused and uncomfortable about breastfeeding before her baby arrives. It's OK to have these thoughts and it's to be expected when we have grown up in the culture that we're in. By acknowledging our feelings and examining them and where they come from, we can start to free ourselves from the restrictions and conflicts they cause in the breastfeeding relationship we have with our baby.

In a world where it's OK to have huge advertisement boards of women in skimpy underwear, but it's frowned upon to breastfeed a baby in a public place, we really have to ask what is going on and why? Perhaps the discomfort comes from the thought of a baby sucking on the breast and nipple which feels like a sexual act. This may lead to feelings of discomfort and confusion, which could present themselves as anger or disgust. These feelings are so at odds with our evolutionary and biological needs.

We are mammals. Mammals are named as such because they have mammary glands to feed their young. Watch any other mammal with their young and they unashamedly allow their offspring free access to the breast. They will allow them to feed wherever and whenever they need to. Even as we look back at our own quite recent human history, we have plenty of art depicting and celebrating babies at the breast. Only as far back as the first half of the last century, it was seen as everyday and normal. The first mammals walked the earth around 160,000,000 years ago and have been breastfeeding ever since. We're pretty good at it. The human species, especially, has increased its population size to extraordinary levels. Breastmilk has been essential to this growth.

Over the last sixty years this has changed, yet babies needs remain the same. I would argue too that women have this need. It's very raw and deep and part of our very evolutionary make-up. It's often something we are not always aware of until our baby arrives. This deep inner need to breastfeed is exacerbated by hormones and our babies' natural reflexes, all of which bring them directly to the breast after birth. So for many there is almost a physical, emotional and moral battle going on when their baby is born. On one side, the stories and experiences picked up throughout life, settled deep within our subconscious, of how babies are fed and of breasts as sexual objects as well as the opinions of society. The other side being the deep need and urge to feed a baby in the way that they want to be fed and with the milk that our bodies are providing. It can become a conflict for many.

Those who support us in early parenthood

Because, for many women, breastfeeding is so brand new and completely unfamiliar, help, support and education for expectant and new parents is vital. In the UK however there are several factors that mean women really struggle to get the help and support they need.

Lack of investment in breastfeeding education for professionals

There is very little breastfeeding education for student doctors, nurses and others who work in perinatal health care. Things are slowly improving in some areas such as midwifery, but when I trained as a paediatric nurse twenty years ago, I had one lecture on infant feeding. Doctors are given little to no opportunity to study the components of breastmilk and how it works physiologically in body. This is a great shame because there is plenty of research available to learn and understand human milk to a deep level.

It is well documented that breastfeeding support is being cut in the UK. The NHS is searching for ways to reduce their expenditure and breastfeeding it seems, is an easy target. We know that this is a very short-sighted cut in funding as research demonstrates how hundreds of millions of pounds could be saved in cancer care alone if most babies were fed breastmilk alone for the first few months.

Medicalisation of infant feeding

Western medicine and science like to measure. They like to be able to measure in units how a baby is doing. So the fact that we can't measure the exact amount of milk that a baby is taking in can feel like a problem to many health professionals. Fortunately there are lots of ways to know if a baby is getting enough milk and I will discuss these in chapter three. Milk flows from each mother and each breast at varying rates and it changes throughout a feed. Babies take in the milk at various speeds, so by timing feeds we don't really have a clear picture of what a baby is getting. The solution is to observe the baby, but many professionals don't have the confidence or the training to know how to do this.

In the UK, giving formula on top of breastfeeding is often the first suggestion from many health professionals when something is not quite right with a baby. It could be that breastfeeding is painful or weight gain is slow. It might be that a baby is unwell in a way that is completely unrelated to breast-feeding, yet adding artificial milk to a baby's diet seems to be the go-to solution for health professionals. This shows a real lack of understanding in the living structure that is breastmilk and the physiology of the human body.

However, a bottle of milk can be measured and being able to know for sure that a baby is having enough milk reassures the health professional that the baby is getting enough food. This can unwittingly cause a variety of problems.

Adding artificial cows-milk based formula to an infant's diet can have short term and long term health consequences.

Whenever babies are fed away from the breast, the breasts make less milk and supply starts to drop.

Mothers start to doubt their ability to feed their baby. They start to doubt their body and their baby's abilities.

Formula milk companies

Artificial milk for human babies is big business. There are plenty of books on the subject if this interests you – see the resources section for further information. However, for the purpose of this chapter, it's important to know that formula companies work hard on advertising to health professionals. They do this in subtle ways that may seem inconsequential, but they ensure that formula milk is in the minds of professionals by:

- advertising their milks in medical journals, wall posters, pens, notepads, other medical tools;

- funding conferences and training days, providing free lunches etc. to health professionals;

- paying for research into infant nutrition;

- meeting with government officials to influence policy.

Formula companies have a history of very strong marketing the world over. It has worked very well in the UK and other countries where marketing has led people to believe that highly processed, powdered cow's milk could be similar to living, ever-adapting human milk.

Lack of breastfeeding experience

Because most mothers now living in the UK have either not breastfed or not breastfed for as long as they wanted to, the healthcare system is full of women who have their own pain and stories from feeding their own babies. Those who have struggled to breastfeed themselves may find it difficult to give impartial and accurate information around breastfeeding to the women in their care. Although not true in every case, this, added to the lack of education in breastfeeding means that women are being given inaccurate, confusing and inconstant advice and information around feeding.

I know this paints a bit of a depressing picture for breastfeeding support in the UK and indeed many other westernised societies. But these are the reasons why it's so important that parents take responsibility for their own breastfeeding education and support. This can be found within the NHS but also within volunteer services and privately. The key for parents is understanding where, how and when they can seek support.

Voluntary breastfeeding support services in the UK

Le Leche league:
https://www.laleche.org.uk/get-support/

The National Breastfeeding Helpline:
https://www.nationalbreastfeedinghelpline.org.uk/

Association of Breastfeeding Mothers:
https://abm.me.uk/get-breastfeeding-support/

National Childbirth Trust (NCT) Helpline: 0300 330 0700

Find an International Board Certified Lactation Consultant (IBCLC) near you:
https://www.lcgb.org/find-an-ibclc/

International breastfeeding support organisations

Le Leche League: https://www.llli.org/get-help/

Lamaze: https://www.lamaze.org/nursing-resources

JOURNALING PROMPTS

When you think about your breasts, how do you feel?

How do you feel about breastfeeding your baby?

How do you feel about breastfeeding in public?

How does your partner feel about breastfeeding?

How do you think your friends and family will respond to you breastfeeding? Why?

Do you have any names or words that you associate with your/your partners breasts?

chapter two
YOUR BRAIN

Our bodies and our brains are intrinsically connected. Our brain uses hormones as messages that rush around our nervous system communicating actions to our body. Our hormones also affect how we feel and some of this we have control over, but much of it we do not – not directly anyway.

Breastfeeding and the workings of our breasts are not immune from this control. In fact it's this very hormone-driven control that makes breastfeeding work. Our body uses two main hormones to produce breastmilk:

Prolactin – tells the milk-making cells to make the milk

Oxytocin – tells the squeezy cells to release the milk

Sounds pretty simple right? This system can work very well and usually does once breastfeeding is established. But lots of different factors can get in the way of these hormones working as they should. Some are physical but many are psychological, and that's the crux of this book really: having an understanding of how our thoughts and our nervous system can affect breastfeeding and how we can use that knowledge to help make our breastfeeding experience a positive one.

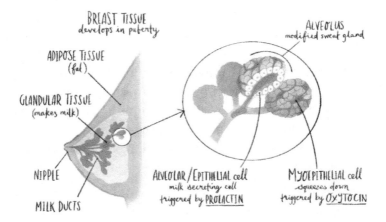

Oxytocin

Oxytocin is my absolute all-time favourite hormone. It's the hormone that rushes around our body when we feel love and closeness to our loved ones. It flows when we cuddle and breathe in our baby's scent. It's the hormone that flows during orgasm. It makes us feel good and it makes us feel relaxed. It also has some important physical functions too. In birth it causes contractions of the uterus and the opening of the cervix. In breastfeeding, the release of milk or let down, as it's usually known.

Oxytocin, however, is a hormone that can be very

sensitive. It flows best in relaxed situations. It is held back in stressful circumstances. It's our autonomic nervous system that controls the release of this hormone and the automatic responses in this are triggered by our feelings and emotions. The more we understand this, the more we can help support an abundance of oxytocin in our bodies. This will not only help the flow of breastmilk but also help you AND your baby to feel more relaxed.

OXYTOCIN FLOWS	OXYTOCIN RESTRICTED
IN A RELAXED ENVIRONMENT	IN A STRESSFUL ENVIRONMENT
WHEN WE FEEL SAFE AND PROTECTED	WHEN WE FEEL WATCHED OR THREATENED
WHEN WE FEEL LOVED AND ENCOURAGED	WHEN WE FEEL CRITICISED
IN QUIET, DIMLY LIT ENVIRONMENT	IN NOISY, BRIGHT ENVIRONMENT
WHEN WE SMILE	WHEN WE FROWN OR GRIMACE
AT HOME	IN AN UNKNOWN ENVIRONMENT
WITH PHYSICAL TOUCH FROM A LOVED ONE	WHEN WE FEEL ALONE OR AFRAID

You can see from the table above that environment, our mood and the people we have around us are central to the flow of oxytocin. It won't always be like this. Once breastfeeding is established and you feel confident, feeding in loud, brightly lit and unknown places is likely to be straight forward. However in the early days and weeks I encourage you to think carefully about the list above.

Stress

We all know what stress feels like. We need stress – in small amounts at least. It actually keeps us safe by alerting us to situations and events that could potentially cause us harm. However, when we are chronically or at least frequently stressed, this releases more of the hormones adrenalin and cortisol than we need. Again, these hormones can help keep us safe, but the secretion of too much of them can have detrimental effects on our physical and mental health.

The issue is that our brains can't really tell the difference between a real life dangerous event or one that has been made up in our mind. We may not even have any awareness of the perceived danger that might start releasing stress hormones into our blood system. The brain and body are completely linked and communicate, for the most part, with each other in a completely automatic way that we have very little control over.

Think about when we have a bad dream and wake up with a thumping heart and pouring with sweat. There was no real danger, but our brain and body certainly thought there was and put the physical functions in place to help keep us safe.

Your autonomic nervous system

This system of controlling our bodily functions to keep us safe is called our autonomic nervous system. The autonomic nervous system has two arms to it. The sympathetic and the parasympathetic nervous system or as I like to call them. Fight/Flight/Freeze and Rest/Digest. The diagram on page 28 shows you how each arm reacts throughout the body in each system.

You can see from looking at this, whilst we are in stress mode or Fight/Flight/Freeze, our body just doesn't work effectively. Rest/Digest is our default setting. And yet so many of us are not living in that state for much of the time.

Birth and the early days of parenting can be stressful for many. If birth went very differently than you expected or if you did not feel in control of the decisions that were made, then this can certainly cause stress.

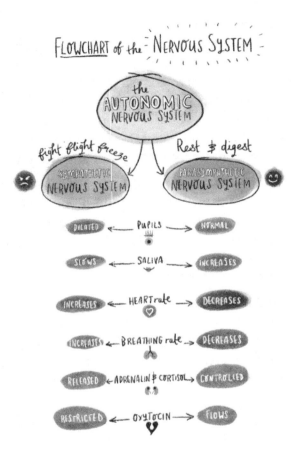

FLOWCHART of the NERVOUS SYSTEM

the AUTONOMIC NERVOUS SYSTEM

fight flight freeze — SYMPATHETIC NERVOUS SYSTEM

Rest & digest — PARASYMPATHETIC NERVOUS SYSTEM

DILATED	← PUPILS →	NORMAL
SLOWS	← SALIVA →	INCREASES
INCREASES	← HEART rate →	DECREASES
INCREASES	← BREATHING rate →	DECREASES
RELEASED	← ADRENALIN & CORTISOL →	CONTROLLED
RESTRICTED	← OXYTOCIN →	FLOWS

When we hold our little baby in our arms there can be so many questions. Everything feels new and we are desperate to get it right. We feel a big responsibility towards this little person that we made and all the information that we're given can feel very overwhelming.

With both birth and the early days of parenting, having an awareness of your autonomic nervous system, and how you can help control it, can have a radical effect on your experience.

As well as influencing your milk ejection reflex (the let-down of your milk), stress also affects your ability to think clearly and to make decisions. It often means that you might struggle to "follow your gut" on something or what you might call your parenting instincts. This is because when we are in survival mode, we can't really connect with our inner wisdom. To do this we need to slow down and soothe our autonomic nervous system.

Learning is also impacted. As you know from chapter one. In our culture, breastfeeding is a learning experience for us. But when we're stressed out, learning is tough. When our brain is in survival mode, learning really isn't top of the agenda – our safety is. It's harder to focus and stay calm, and patience is not something that comes easily when we're in Fight/Flight/Freeze mode. With breastfeeding, and actually parenting generally, we need a whole lot of patience!

As well as making it difficult to connect with ourselves, being in the Fight/Flight/Freeze mode makes it difficult to connect with others around us, our partners and our baby too. It's impossible to relax and enjoy being with others when we're stressed out and anxious. Babies pick up on this right from the start, so learning some ways to get on top of stress benefits everyone.

Relaxation

So have I convinced you yet? Are you wondering how you can make a start on gaining some control over your autonomic nervous system and spend more time in that Rest/Digest mode? I'm really hoping you answered yes, because it's much simpler than we might imagine. In fact, I bet most of you reading this already have a pretty good idea at ways that you can help yourself to become calmer and more relaxed. The key is actually doing it and doing it regularly. The more that we consciously help our body and our mind to relax, the less time we will spend in Fight/Flight/ Freeze mode.

The tools themselves are broken down in the later chapters. They are all simple and manageable. Try them out and see which ones work best for you. Relaxation is something that we become better at the more we do it. If practised daily, you will start to see shifts, pretty quickly. Research shows that with just 10 consecutive days of regular practice of deep muscle relaxation, not only our minds but our bodies are changed. That on a cellular level our health is improved. Isn't that amazing? And we're not talking hours of sitting cross legged on a mediation mat here! Just 10 minutes a day will do.

And if you don't have time for that then breathing exercises can be done at any time and anywhere. If the thought of deep muscle relaxation feels intimidating right now then start with some breathing exercises and see how they work for you.

Learning a skill

In chapter one we talked about how building up subconscious pictures is one of the ways that we learn. If we lack realistic pictures of breastfeeding, then we're starting with very little knowledge and we have more to learn than parents who grew up in a breastfeeding culture. Fortunately, babies are born with the reflexes they need to latch on to the breast themselves with very little assistance. However, medicalised birthing practices and a general lack of understanding and experience in normal breast-feeding behaviour means that babies are rarely given the chance to have a go on their own.

Therefore the sooner you can start the process of learning the skill of breastfeeding, the faster your learning will be. To become automatic at something takes time. Building muscle memory takes 2-4 weeks of repeating a task in a certain way. However breastfeeding looks and feels different for everyone, so finding the way that works for you and your baby is an important first step. Over time, as you grow in confidence, you will be able to start latching your baby on more quickly and before long you'll be doing it without thinking.

By reading this book you've already made a conscious decision to learn more about breastfeeding. It's a great first step. The next chapter introduces you further to how breastfeeding works, how to attach your baby to the breast and what to expect from your little one when they arrive. Going to a breastfeeding class or doing one online, would kick-start your learning even more. However, there are other ways that you can start building up that subconscious picture of breastfeeding. Here's a list:

1. Go to your local breastfeeding group and ask questions – they love to meet pregnant women.

2. Visit friends or family members who breastfeed.

3. Read further books – find the list of recommendations in the next chapter.

4. Follow #breastfeeding on Instagram and Facebook to start seeing breastfeeding a lot more on your social media feeds.

5. Build an online or real-life vision board with pictures and affirmations.

Mindset
Negative pictures and negative ideas around breastfeeding can really affect your breastfeeding experience. If you explored some of the journaling prompts from the last chapter then you may have already started to identify some of the thought patterns you have that are related to breastfeeding. The good news is that you can alter these negative

thought processes into more positive ones. Your brain's ability to do this is called neuroplasticity and modern science is teaching us more and more about our ability to change and grow the connections in our brain.

Mindset can have a huge impact on your ability to learn as well, so it's well worth popping to chapter four to find out more about how you can alter your mindset using the power of positive affirmations.

JOURNALING PROMPTS

If you were to give yourself a score for how stressed or relaxed you are most of the time what would it be?

1 = relaxed almost all of the time
10= stressed almost all of the time.

How do you know when you're stressed? Are you able feel it in your body? If so, where?

What do you like to do to relax?

How aften are you able to do this at the moment?

Moving onto your thoughts and feelings, do you have many recurring negative or critical thoughts? If so, write them below.

chapter three
how BREASTFEEDING WORKS

Now that you understand how as a society our belief systems around infants and infant feeding are shaped, I'm sure you can appreciate the importance of knowing how the breastfeeding body works. In historical times, this knowledge would have passed down the generations. It would have been picked up intrinsically as you watched your siblings, cousins and friends' babies breastfeed. Without realising it, you would already have built up a rich, visual understanding of breastfeeding and in turn a very different level of trust in your body and your baby.

So without this "knowing" in ourselves, our families and our health system, for at least the last generation or two, we absolutely must take the responsibility of learning how to breastfeed upon ourselves. There are already a huge number of amazing books that are dedicated to this topic. Here is overview, but I highly recommend enhancing your knowledge further. Here are my favourite resources for further education in breastfeeding:

Online Course:

The Mindful Breastfeeding School
www.themindfulbreastfeedingschool.com

Books:

The Womanly Art of Breastfeeding (8th Ed) Le Leche League

The Positive Breastfeeding Book, Amy Brown

You've Got it in You: A Positive Guide to Breast-feeding, Emma Pickett

CROSS CRADLE

It's also worth finding out if there is a face-to-face breastfeeding class near to you. You could start by asking the health professionals who are supporting you such as your midwife, health visitor or paediatrician. Your local breastfeeding volunteer support group or local antenatal teachers may also run classes.

The breast

It can help to think of the inside of a breast as a bit like a broccoli. Inside are milk-making "florets". They are bunches of sacs that make and hold the milk and are called lobules or alveoli. Milk ducts stem from each sac and when the milk is squeezed out – during "let-down" – the milk travels down these ducts which are like the narrow stems of the broccoli. These come out of the holes at the end of the nipple. The nipple can be thought of as the thick part of the broccoli stem.

Interestingly, a woman's breasts have a varying number of alveoli ducts and openings in the nipple. This is likely to have an impact on the flow of her milk. The amount of milk that can be stored also varies from women to woman. Ultrasounds have found that the number of openings in the nipple can range from 4 to 18. The storage capacity of each breast is unrelated to the size of a breast as the amount of fat and glandular tissue varies so much. Lobules can be found in surprising places meaning that those with smaller breasts may have quite a good storage capacity and those with larger breasts could have less in the way of alveoli (glandular tissue) but more fatty tissue.

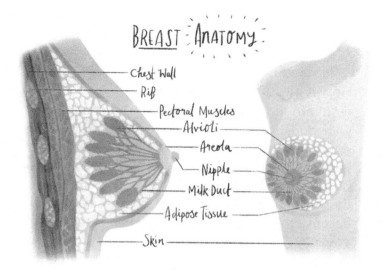

Understanding the varying breast anatomy between women can be really helpful when breastfeeding starts. It helps us to understand how breastfeeding is going to look different from one woman and baby to the next. As you have no idea what the inside anatomy of your breast looks like, you can't know right now, how your milk will flow or how much milk you will be able to store at one time. This is one of the reasons why timing feeds or timing the intervals between feeds can be a dangerous game. The woman who has fewer alveoli and fewer milk duct openings in her nipple is likely to need to feed her baby for longer at each feed and potentially more often than a woman with a large milk storage capacity and 15 milk duct openings. How do you know which one you will be? You don't. Not to start with anyway. This is where you need to start trusting your baby and following their lead. I'll talk about this a bit later in the chapter.

How it all starts – colostrum
From around the beginning of the second trimester your body starts to make colostrum. Colostrum is a gold coloured, thick and sticky milk that is the first your baby will receive. It's packed full of immune factors and all the other things your baby needs in those first days. It is produced in very small amounts because that is all that your baby needs to start with. You may not even see it due to its viscose consistency. Interestingly, your colostrum changes throughout your pregnancy, to suit the age of your baby. Therefore, if your baby is born early it will have colostrum ready for exactly the stage that they are at.

During the third stage of labour, when your placenta detaches from the wall of your uterus, a sharp drop in the hormone progesterone sends a message for your breasts to start changing the colostrum into mature milk. This is the more watery and lighter coloured milk that we think of when we think of breastmilk. This transition takes a few days and varies from woman to woman. Sometimes milk will start to change after 24 or 48 hours. For many it is three days and for some it might take longer. Later on I'll talk about the signs you can look out for to be sure that your milk is changing.

The first hour after birth

Studies show that babies who breastfeed in the first hour after birth are likely to breastfeed for longer overall. Therefore, if you can have your baby skin to skin with you after the birth, then this will help your milk supply and your baby in the early hours of their life. Skin to skin has so many benefits. Here's a list:

Why skin to skin?

- Brain connections (neural pathways) are created faster and in a normal pattern when babies start off their life skin to skin.

- Mothers also have new neural pathways being formed when they hold their baby after the birth.

- It aids temperature regulations for babies.

- Babies can hear your heartbeat, breath and bowel sounds – familiar sounds.

- Babies can hear your voice, which is also familiar to them.

- The smell of your colostrum is similar to the taste of amniotic fluid.

- It's a gentle transition into the outside world.

- Babies have instant access to the breast for when they are ready to feed.

- You can watch for feeding signals – mouthing, routing, licking and moving their head from side to side.

- It helps you to rest after the birth.
- Both you and your baby will be more relaxed.
- It helps oxytocin to flow and therefore your milk to release (let-down).

If you are unable to be skin to skin with your baby then your partner or family member can do it instead.

The first hour after birth can sometimes be called the golden hour. An hour when this skin to skin is prioritised and all other things can wait to get done. This includes weighing your baby, dressing them, your shower or wash. You may want to write these things down in your birth plan or preferences list so that your care providers know that it's important to you.

Some babies are born early and need support from medical equipment and are therefore unable to be skin to skin after the birth. In these circumstances, skin to skin can happen as soon as your baby is ready and most neonatal departments will facilitate you to do this as soon as possible. It's never too late to hold your baby next to your skin in this way. It has so many positive effects, including increasing your milk supply and is the perfect way to bond with your little one.

LAID BACK

NATURAL BREASTFEEDING

Balancing out your milk supply – trusting your baby

As your milk starts to change from colostrum to the more watery mature milk, you may notice that your breasts start to grow in size. They may become engorged, swollen or painful. This doesn't happen to everyone so don't worry if you don't experience this. At this point your body and its hormones are fully focused on milk making and the best things to do is feed your baby as much as possible.

Babies have tiny tummies at birth. They fill up quickly and empty quickly, so feeding frequently keeps your baby and your boobs happy. Most babies will feed between 8 and 12 times in 24 hours in the first three months. Many will feed more. But it's important that you follow your baby's lead as this helps your body work out exactly how much milk to make.

The milk-making cells of the alveola have a system that starts to respond to the amount of milk your baby removes from the breast. It takes around six weeks of communication between your baby and your breasts to establish the correct supply. If you think back to the beginning of the chapter where I talked about how different the anatomy of each breast can be, you'll understand why it's important to be led by your baby as they are the best guide to whether they have had enough milk or not.

Feeding cues are the best things to look out for to know when your baby is hungry. By picking these up early you will reach your baby before they become stressed and a relaxed baby makes all the difference when you're learning to breastfeed. Trying to stretch out the time between feeds or assuming that your baby should only feed 3 hourly or 4 hourly could easily start to cause problems for the mum with a smaller milk storage capacity. "Missing" feeds in this way will mean that your body will start making less milk and will not be able to keep up with the amount of milk your baby needs. Trusting that your baby will take what they need will make a huge difference to how you feel in the early days and weeks.

In some circumstances babies aren't able to tell us every time that they need to feed, so there's a few other signs that we need to keep an eye out for too.

Wet nappies – Should be frequent and increasing with each day after birth – 6 in 24 hours by day 5.

Dirty nappies – Once the meconium has passed after birth babies who are having enough breastmilk will open their bowels at least 3 times a day.

Weight – Almost all babies will lose weight after birth but after day 5 a baby who is getting enough milk will start to gain weight again.

Behaviour – Your baby's behaviour can also be an indicator for whether they are getting enough milk.

The very sleepy baby
There are lots of reasons that your baby might be very sleepy. Birth in the Western world often involves medical intervention, which can lead to babies being extra sleepy on arrival.

The following factors may mean your baby is wanting to sleep and not feed:

- Induction of labour – especially before any signs of labour have occurred.

- Caesarean birth – as above.

- Drugs in labour.

- Low blood sugars – this is especially common for babies of mothers with gestational diabetes or diabetes.

- Premature birth.

- Low birth weight.

In a normal problem-free scenario, babies will have a breastfeed in the first hour after birth and then have a long sleep to recover from the birth. After this sleep they will start to feed frequently.

In situations where a baby is extra sleepy and not waking often for feeds, they will need some encouragement to take breastmilk. Remember the guide of 8-12 feeds every 24 hours? This can be used to judge when you should be offering your baby the breast. Most babies will feed every 1 to 3 hours at this point. Although it may feel more often than that to you!

You're going to think I'm obsessed with skin to skin, and you'd be right! It really is a wonderful solution to any issues in the early weeks. If your baby is sleepy then keep them on your chest if you can, in their nappy but otherwise naked next to your naked chest. That way they will be able to smell your milk and it will help encourage them to find the breast and feed.

Some babies may need a little more than this and a little bit of expressed colostrum rubbed on their lips or expressed onto a spoon and given to them, can help increase their blood sugars and encourage them

to wake and feed more. If you're wondering about hand expressing then go to the resources page for more.
http://mindfulbreastfeeding.co.uk/book-resources/

The very unsettled baby

Sometimes babies are very unhappy between feeds. If your baby never seems satisfied after a feed and is crying a lot, then it's time to get some support. On the second day and night of life it can be very normal for your baby to cluster feed – and want to be at the breast a lot. If this continues and you feel like your baby is never satisfied, then get support from a breastfeeding specialist who will help you to assess if your baby is getting enough milk. See the resources at the back for finding somebody near you.

Hormones

As mentioned in the previous chapter there are two main hormones that are connected with lactation.

Prolactin – Tells the milk making cells to make more milk

Oxytocin – triggers the release of the milk from the alveoli (let down)

You already know from chapter two how sensitive oxytocin can be. Stress, anxiety, fear and feelings of being judged can all affect whether your milk lets down or not, and how quickly this happens. The good news is that for many of us, just holding or being near our baby floods our body with oxytocin. This is the main reason why milk often lets down more easily when breastfeeding than it does when expressing. It's also the reason that skin to skin works so well.

At night prolactin levels are higher meaning that most milk is made at this time. In the morning many women will wake up and feel like they have an abundance of milk that then slowly reduces throughout the day. This is completely normal and we know that it's important for babies to have milk from all of those times of day but that in the evenings the less voluminous milk (but not in nutrients and immune factors) is a little bit harder for babies to remove from the breast and they may feed more frequently and for longer at these times – called cluster feeding.

Again, listen to what your baby is telling you. If they are feeding more than you expected but their nappy output, behaviour and weight gain are all OK then everything IS OK. Often we are given so many confusing messages from others around us. Expectations of family members and professionals, not to mention the internet, can leave us feeling like we are getting it wrong!

A read of chapter six, Trust, might be helpful if you're feeling overwhelmed by all the information. And chapter five, Relaxation, is full of tools that are there to help you filter out the noise and find your own parenting path.

Latch and pain in breastfeeding

I'm sure you've heard it said time and time again that latch is important when it comes to breastfeeding, but you're probably also wondering why something so natural can sound so technical. Well in many parts of Western society our natural instincts, when it comes to feeding and caring for our young, have been damaged. Babies are born with all the reflexes necessary to breastfeed, but our medicalised birth practices, modern expectations on babies and bottle feeding culture has meant that as new parents we are starting off on the back foot. Because of the general lack of knowledge, education and experience around breastfeeding, new mothers do need to be taught what breastfeeding looks and feels like, and a really great place to start is talking about the latch.

I like video resources for learning about latch – visuals are especially useful I find. You can find some great ones on my website resources page. http://mindfulbreastfeeding.co.uk/book-resources/

A key thing to remember is that for a baby to feed well and for breastfeeding to be comfortable, your nipple needs to be near the back of your baby's mouth. Therefore they need to take in quite a bit of breast with an open-wide mouth. Feel in the roof of your mouth with your tongue. The front of your palate is hard and sometimes ribbed. As you go further back into your mouth the hard palate changes into the soft and this is where in your baby's mouth the nipple needs to go. Not only does it mean comfort for you but also efficient feeding.

Many people say that breastfeeding hurts in the beginning and that it's normal, that you just need to feed through it and it will get better. The problem with this kind of advice is that firstly pain is very subjective. We all feel it differently and we are able to cope with it differently. Breastfeeding pain means that something isn't quite right. In the beginning it's likely to be that you and your baby haven't quite learnt the best way to do it yet. Given time, yes it may get better, but it might not. So I always encourage mothers to seek help straight away if breastfeeding hurts.

If the thought of having your baby on the breast fills you with dread before every feed or if the pain is toe-curling or if there is any damage at all, then seeing a breastfeeding specialist is a matter of urgency. Check out chapter seven, Support, for more.

Positioning

I'm not going to list positions here as there is such a wide range of positions and they are slightly different for each parent and baby. It's all about finding one that is comfortable for you and I hope that the artwork in this book gives you some inspiration and some ideas to try. Because body shapes of Mother and baby vary so much, positions will look slightly different for everyone anyway! The most important thing is to find a position that you are comfortable in and in which your baby can get a large mouthful of breast. If you have nipple pain then changing positions can be a great thing to try initially. There are a few useful tips that can help your baby get a deep mouthful of breast:

- Make sure their body is in a straight line from head to bottom. Any twists in the neck can make latching on difficult.

- Have their tummy flat against your body. Babies love to be held close and when the front of their body is right next to yours it helps their feeding reflexes to kick in.

- Keep your hand away from the back of their head. It can make them feel restricted and stop them from wanting to open wide.

- Aim your nipple to their nose or just below it. This encourages them to open up wide. If you try to put your nipple in their mouth they will simply suck on the nipple and wont take a mouthful of breast.

Remember that being relaxed makes all the difference to breastfeeding, so make sure you're comfortable first and then bring your baby to your breast. If you're relaxed in body, even if not in mind just at this moment, your baby will pick up on this and it will be easier to help them to breastfeed. More on this in chapter five.

CRADLE
HOLD

The first weeks

Over time, as you and your baby find comfortable ways to breastfeed, your body and your baby will communicate to find the balance in your breastmilk production. In each of the milk-making cells little receptors are measuring how much milk is being removed from your breast. The receptors then use the hormone prolactin to either turn up or turn down milk production.

The more milk you can produce for your baby in the first six weeks, the more flexibility you will have with your milk supply later on. That's why feeding your baby as often as they ask is a great way of ensuring you have a good supply throughout your breastfeeding journey. Each time your breasts feel engorged they turn down milk production in the milk-making cells and when your breasts are emptier, they ramp up the milk making.

If you let your baby guide this production process, then things will go a lot smoother. There are certain things that can get in the way that it's important to be aware of:

- Stretching out times between feeds – This can lead to your body not making enough milk for your baby.

- Using a dummy/pacifier – Dummies meet the sucking needs of a baby and you may miss their feeding cues, meaning that they could go longer between feeds than they need to. This again can reduce your milk supply. Having lots of warm cuddles with other family members or visitors can have the same effect on your supply. So keep an eye out for these accidental ways of missing breastfeeds.

- Pumping – If you express milk as well as feeding your baby responsively, you're telling your body to make more milk than your baby needs. For some women this can cause an over-supply, which is an issue for some babies. It can make them windy and for some, make them vomit. A fuller breast will have a faster flow and some babies struggle with it and take in air as they gulp the milk down. If you know you want to pump to perhaps build up a supply of expressed frozen milk, then it can be helpful to wait until you feel your milk supply and breastfeeding are established. Once you start, finding a routine where you pump the same number of times a day can help your body to know what's going on. Once a day is enough for anyone who wants to give the odd feed away from the breast.

KOALA hold

Special circumstances

This chapter is about what breastfeeding looks like for most people under normal circumstances. Of course there's a million and one variations on this. But by having a clear idea of how breastmilk production actually works, you can find breastfeeding-friendly solutions to most tricky situations.

Sometimes there is an organic or surgical reason why mothers are unable to produce enough milk for their baby. Sometimes babies are unable to transfer milk well because they are premature, are unwell or have oral ties or other physical difficulties. With any of these situations it will help to have support from a breastfeeding specialist who can assess what is going on and help you to devise a feeding plan that will support your breastfeeding wishes. See chapter seven, Support, for more on this.

The three things to remember if breastfeeding isn't going well are:

1. Ensure that your baby is being fed enough. Preferably this will be with your own milk from your breast or your milk pumped and given in a different way (cup, spoon, syringe, bottle or with an at-breast-supplementer are all options and can be discussed with your breastfeeding support person). Donated human milk and formula milk are also options if you are unable to provide the milk your baby needs at this time.

2. Ensure that you are regularly removing milk from your breast. Even if your baby isn't feeding at the breast or feeding only a little, your body needs to be given the message to keep making milk otherwise it will stop. Aim to express as many times as your baby would be feeding – at least 8 times in 24 hours in the beginning.

3. When your milk is at the colostrum stage, hand expressing can yield the most and is something

which I recommend everyone learns how to do in pregnancy. Anything that is expressed, even if it's the tiniest of drops, can be given to your baby.

Once your milk starts to change you may want to switch to using a pump. If you are pumping a lot then using a good quality electric pump or hiring a hospital-grade pump will make all the difference.

If you're expressing, make sure you read chapter five, Relaxation, for lots of tips on increasing the amount of milk you are able to pump.

Find someone to support you who understands how to protect your milk supply and helps you to find breastfeeding-friendly ways to feed your baby. If you do not have direct access to someone see the resources listed at the back of this book. Or go to the resources webpage.

http://mindfulbreastfeeding.co.uk/book-resources/

JOURNALING PROMPTS

After reading this chapter what are now your expectations for breastfeeding?

What more do you want to know and where do you plan to find this information or support?

Do you have any new worries or concerns about breastfeeding your baby?

Write down any questions you have for your care providers/health professionals here.

chapter four
POSITIVE SELF-TALK

Our brains are amazing things, it's what makes us human. But with the stresses and strains of modern life, and whilst we spend so much time in our sympathetic nervous system, many of our thoughts are negative, and this has a profound effect on us.

We have tens of thousands of thoughts a day and up to 80 percent of those are thought to be negative and 95 percent are believed to be repeated thoughts (National Science Foundation, 2005). The good news is that we do have some control over these thoughts: we can change what we're thinking and feeling and we can change our brain activity. Neuroplasticity is the way that our mind adapts to different circumstances. It's how we can learn and alter our mindset – in fact it's the opposite to "mind-set". We have the ability to alter the way our brain works through our thoughts and feelings.

Thinking positive thoughts can actually change the activity in several parts of the brain, which in turn increases self-esteem, helps us to cope in difficult situations and makes us feel good. Affirmations are a way of making these alterations in our mind. If repeated often enough, positive thoughts can re-write the thoughts in our conscious and subconscious mind that take up so much of our thinking time.

Our inner critic

Having awareness of our negative thoughts isn't always easy, but I assure you that even if you feel you don't have any negative thoughts about yourself, they will be there somewhere. Some of us are acutely aware of our stream of thoughts, to the extent where it can lead to anxiety or depression. For others it can take a while to become familiar with recognising the negative thought patterns. As you start to use some of the Mindfulness techniques in this book, you are likely to become more aware of your inner critic. Your inner critic is that voice that says negative things about you, to you. It's often repetitive and, although it's your brain's way of keeping you safe, it keeps you from doing the things you would like to do. It knocks your confidence and stops you believing in yourself.

For example, if your inner critic frequently tells you that you are going to have a bad breastfeeding experience, that story is likely to be repeated over and over again in different ways throughout your pregnancy. Perhaps your own mother had problems breastfeeding or you witnessed a family member or friend have a terrible time. You may really want to breastfeed, but you have self-doubt running around in your mind. Lots of "what ifs" and perhaps an inability to trust in your body.

When it comes to your little one being born, your brain will look for links in your reality to the messages that your subconscious has been telling you. Someone who believes that they will not have enough milk, will be looking for evidence of that without even realising it. If you believe that breastfeeding will be hard for you. Then you are more likely to notice the bits that feel hard than the bits that feel easy.

Affirmations can be a tool that enables you to have a more positive experience, helping with your levels of confidence, self-belief and trust in your body and your baby. They may not stop actual challenges arising. But they can have an impact on your outlook and how you deal with any difficulties as well as how you feel about yourself and your baby at this time.

Now that you have explored your views and beliefs around infant feeding you can start to use them to build up a positive self-supportive foundation that you can use when your baby arrives. So often I see brand new parents, especially mothers, who are full of fear and anxiety, who are worried about every move they make with their baby and constantly feel they are getting it wrong. I think that this is especially true when they have experienced a difficult birth or had ongoing fertility problems.

In this modern age we are so used to being able to control every aspect of our lives. We are taught that if we strive for something enough, if we work hard enough, if we do the work ourselves that we can have what we want, when we want it. With most new mothers being in their late 20s to 40s, we have built up successful careers and have worked hard and seen results. We've orchestrated our achievements and striven for success time and time again. And yes, intention, preparation and knowledge help us a huge amount with pregnancy, childbirth and parenting. But with knowledge, often comes fear. And to exacerbate the fear, comes the issue that we can't control everything when it comes to making and raising babies.

Now I would argue that we can actually guide our journey more than we think, and that's where this chapter comes in. I'd like you to think about guiding your journey, rather than controlling it. I think it's helpful. We do have power over our emotions and our feelings and we do have control over our reactions to situations. How we react can change everything. For ourselves and for those around us, especially our babies.

How to use affirmations

The more we say positive affirmations to ourselves the more likely we are going to feel and believe them. There are several ways of using them:

- Write them out each morning into a journal or on a piece of paper.

- Write them onto cards and put them in prominent place around your house – see resources section.

- Look at the cards and repeat them to yourself regularly – first thing on the morning and last thing at night can work well.

- Record them onto a voice note and listen to them as you go to sleep – see resources section.

- Put a favourite one as a screen saver on your phone.

- Write one on a sheet of paper in a colourful font or in bubble writing that you can colour in and put up in your home.

- Stand in front of a mirror and say them to yourself.

How to write affirmations

Affirmations are short positive statements about ourselves that we repeat to ourselves to change the way that we feel by over-riding some of the negative thought patterns that we have. Now that you have been uncovering some of the thought patterns that you have around feeding, it would be a great time to write some affirmations so that you can start feeling positive as soon as possible about your breastfeeding and parenting journey.

I have added a space at the end of this chapter so that you can write some of your own affirmations. But before you get started there are four basic rules for creating affirmations.

1 Keep them positive

We're talking positive language here, so saying I am or I do. If we start saying what we are not or what we're not going to do, then we focus on that instead of the thing we do want.

2 Keep it in the present tense

There are two schools of thought here, and there is some evidence coming to light that affirmations stated in the future may work better for some people.

However, I and many others who teach affirmations for positive self talk, find being in the here and now works well. When using affirmations we want our mind and our body to believe it's happening now, so keeping it in the present tense works well. The more we say the affirmation the more it becomes like a little mantra, so that when we actually do come to that moment in our lives the words will come automatically to us.

Saying "I will" or "I hope" plants a seed of self-doubt in our minds – the possibility that it might happen one day or indeed not happen at all. If we want to affirm a feeling or an action we need it to be a sure thing and we need to believe that it is going to happen.

3 Keep it in the first person

It's an internal voice we're aiming for, not a statement about ourselves. We want to hear and believe it, internalise it and then feel and live it. Use "I" or "Me".

4 Make it not too far from your reality

There's no point making an affirmation that repels you. It can't be something that is impossible. Think baby steps and slowly changing your mindset on something that feels big. An affirmation can and should feel like a stretch but if it's too far away from how you feel right now, then you're unlikely to believe in it.

Writing affirmations, if you've never done it before, can feel tricky and unnatural. It takes practice and as you're writing out anxieties, worries and negative thoughts about yourself, strong emotions may surface. This is OK, you're uncovering thought processes and stories that you may not even have been aware of until now. This stuff is emotional and changing the status quo of our thought patterns can feel uncomfortable and scary. Give yourself the space and time to do it and be super kind to yourself as well. I find when doing this type of work that the affirmation:

I love and accept myself

can feel really comforting and allows me to be honest about whatever else comes up.

If you don't quite feel ready to write your own affirmations, then I have a list here that you may find helpful. They are all breastfeeding related. Have a look through and see if any resonate with you. The ones that do can be used in any of the ways listed above. They are also available as printouts on my website and in card packs that you can buy from my website.

I trust my body and my baby

I ask for help when I need it

I trust my instincts

I take it one feed at a time

I am the best Mum for my baby

My baby gets exactly what they need from my milk

I feel fully supported in my decisions

I feel relaxed and calm as I feed my baby

What happens in my breastfeeding journey is between me and my baby

I am confident in my body's ability to feed my baby

I believe in my body's ability to grow my baby's brain

I nourish myself so I can nourish my baby

My body is capable of amazing things

As I see what my body is capable of, I fall more and more in love with it

My body knows how to nourish my baby

I trust my baby to know how much milk they need and my body follows their lead

My body is capable of magical things

I love myself so that I can love others

I control what I can and let go of what I can't

I take it one day at a time

This breastfeeding stuff gets easier everyday

I am grateful for what my body is able to do

JOURNALING PROMPTS

Have a go at writing your own affirmations:

Think of something that is worrying you or is on your mind about breastfeeding or parenting.

Problem or worry

Remembering the four rules of writing affirmations on the previous pages, have a go at writing a positive statement that will help you to think about this differently. Something that gives you confidence and makes you feel better about things when you say it to yourself.

My affirmation

Problem or worry

My affirmation

Problem or worry

My affirmation

Problem or worry

My affirmation

chapter five
RELAXATION

Being someone who is naturally on the go, relaxation doesn't come easy to me. I used to find the idea of relaxation boring or a waste of time. I would perhaps watch the odd movie (I would usually fall asleep) and I do enjoy nothing more than lying in the sun with a good book .... although those days are few and far between since becoming a mother. I liked the idea of meditation and have always loved a shavasna at the end of yoga sessions, but again these were rare moments. Most of the time, the default me is rushing around, trying to fit as much into my day as possible. Seeing friends, taking the children to classes or school, working, preparing meals, cleaning up the house – there's always something to do! Sound familiar?

In 2015 my body went on a protest and made me ill. I had no choice but to take a stark look at my life and all that I was trying to fit in. I didn't start getting better until I made some major lifestyle changes. So what's the link? Why do our bodies and our minds need to relax? And what on earth does this have to do with breastfeeding?

If you have already read chapter two you have already read a little about the autonomic nervous system. This system has two arms to it. The first is our parasympathetic nervous system which is our default setting. When we're in this "mode" we feel good or maybe just neutral, content and OK with the world. It's likely that we're breathing normally – slowly and deep into our lungs. Our body is relaxed and importantly, inside of our body, everything is functioning well. Our gut is absorbing and moving as it should. As we breathe in fully our lungs take in and transfer a good amount of oxygen to our blood stream. This in turn is circulated right around our body and to every place that needs it.

If you're making milk, your body will be able to

respond to the circulation of the hormones present. When we're relaxed oxytocin can flow. Oxytocin is the hormone that gives your body the signal to release the milk from your breasts. It triggers the squeezing cells that surround each milk-making sac (alveoli), which push out the milk into the milk ducts.

Our body and our mind like it when we're relaxed and in our parasympathetic system. Studies have shown that even on a cellular level our bodies are functioning at their best. So for both our body and for our mind, knowing how to relax is actually essential.

The other arm of our autonomic nervous system is the sympathetic nervous system which is our heightened state of alert. As mentioned in chapter two, we need this arm of the nervous system to keep us safe. Imagine you are about to step out into the road but a car suddenly comes along. Our nervous system alarms and our brain ensures that our body reacts quickly by making us jump out of the way, quite automatically. This is also called our Fight/|Flight/Freeze system. To keep us safe from danger the autonomic nervous system:

- sends blood and oxygen to our lungs and heart;
- opens up our pupils to let in light;
- dries up our saliva.

But it also:

- releases cortisol and adrenalin;

- slows the production of oxytocin;

- slows down the digestive system by reducing blood flow to the area, reducing muscle function and drying up secretions needed for effective digestion.

So in our everyday life, not just in early parenthood, it's important that we try and keep ourselves in the Rest/Digest part of the nervous system (parasympathetic) which should be our default setting. This is so that our digestive system and other areas of our body can work as they should. We need our Fight/Flight/Freeze mode but only when we're in danger.

In our modern world, for many of us, to get back into being in our parasympathetic nervous system we are going to have to consciously make the time and space to relax. When I say relax, what I mean is deep muscle relaxation where we relax our mind as well as our body. Where we slow our mind down and stop focusing on our thoughts so much.

Our thoughts

One of the things that put me off meditation in the past, was that I believed that I needed to empty my mind for long periods of time. This felt so far from the busy mind that I experience day to day, and like an impossible task. But as I started to meditate regularly, I discovered that I could, over time, train myself to stop focusing on my thoughts instead of not having any at all – after all I'm not aiming to be the Dali Lama, just give my nervous system a bit of a rest! When I make time to relax/meditate I allow the thoughts to be there. I can acknowledge them, but let them go whilst I bring my focus back to something else. Some people like to think about their thoughts as clouds passing across the sky. Their thoughts coming into their mind and out again, not affecting them, but simply floating through, quite unattached.

When you're learning how to relax, having a focus or an anchor can be a very helpful way to stop you getting caught up with your thoughts. Many relaxations use the breath in this way. It's a useful thing to focus on because it's something you are doing anyway. It's so automatic that we are usually unaware of it anyway. The bonus of focusing on the breath is that by breathing well we're not only quieting the mind but also oxygenating our body in a wonderful way. Breathing oxygen right down into our lungs benefits all of the organs of our body, giving them a good dose of oxygenated blood.

Other things that can help with focus are music, a candle flame, an image or even a scent. Anything really, that relaxes you and that you can easily bring your focus back to.

How to
As with anything, the more that you can practise relaxation the easier it becomes. If you're pregnant, now is a really good time to start. If your baby is

already here, don't worry! It can be more challenging to find the time but you will notice the benefits really quickly. Consistency is key, so think about where you could routinely add some relaxation time into your day or evening. If you're new to this then starting off with a short guided relaxation is perfect. Something between 5 and 15 minutes long. You have access to five guided relaxations that I have written, so go to the website and have a look.

The "Short Relaxation" is only 5 minutes, so whether you're pregnant or you have a baby, schedule in the time and try and make it daily for the next ten days. Research tells us that ten consecutive days of deep muscle relaxation makes changes to your body on a cellular level, improving your health and wellbeing. I recommend keeping notes on how you feel each day. You can either buy a beautiful and inspiring new notebook for this or you can use the spaces set out at the end of this chapter. Make the commitment and you'll soon feel the difference that creating this small amount of time for yourself makes.

Breathing

A really great place to start with relaxation is becoming more aware of your breath. Breathing exercises may sound a bit cliché, especially if you're pregnant. But they're not just for labour. Breathing techniques are for life. And take it from me, when you're a parent, remembering your breathing techniques when you're having one of those moments, is a complete gamechanger – even when your baby is 12 years old!

Breathing properly and deeply calms down the nervous system, floods your body with oxygen and gets you out of your Fight/Flight/Freeze response, allowing you to think more clearly and respond in a more positive and helpful way to any situation. The beauty of using breathing techniques around your little ones is that children are always watching and copying what we're doing. You're teaching them emotional regulation from a young age whilst helping yourself and the situation you're in.

The beauty of breathing techniques is that you always have your lungs with you wherever you go and it's something that you can do discreetly. Focused breathing can be done at any time and anywhere. Below are three of my favourites all of which are very simple and easy to follow.

The steady breath
Breathe in through your nose and count to 5.

Breathe out of your mouth for the same length of time, counting to 5.

After three of these you'll feel calmer already.

Belly breathing
Put your hand on your abdomen and as you breathe in, feel your belly expanding.

As you breathe out feel it move back. You can make

a sighing or whooshing noise as you breath out for a more cleansing breath.

When you feel your abdomen moving as you breathe you know that you're breathing right down into the bottom of your lungs. This maximises the amount of oxygen that your body is able to take in, transferring it to all of the organs that need it.

Calming breath

Breathe in for a count of 4.

Hold your breath for a count of 7.

Breathe out for a breath of 8.

When doing this breath for the first time, you may find yourself getting a little light headed, so just stick to 3 or 4 of these at the beginning and see how you feel.

Focus

One of the best things about taking a few seconds out to do some breathing exercises is that it means that you have to concentrate on what you're doing for that time. It gives you a focus away from the busyness of your mind. There are other ways that we can slow down and quieten the mind and enjoy some relaxation. A very effective way is to follow a guided relaxation and the rest of this chapter is devoted to that. But it's not always possible to do this with babies or children around.

Focusing on anything that feels restful or positive can

be a mindful task. Learning a new skill for example, is usually something that we have to concentrate on, and therefore quietens the chatter in our minds. This might be learning a new craft, doing exercise, dancing or singing. Yoga is a wonderful route to Mindfulness and relaxation. As well as concentrating on what you are doing, you also regulate the breath and in most sessions, relax at the end.

Hearing your inner guide

In these fast-paced, information-overloaded times, it can be hard to believe that we have all of the answers inside of us, but we really do. We all have innate parenting instincts and a connection to our baby, long before they're born. Even if you don't feel this connection, I promise you it is there and your baby feels it too.

Finding ways to relax and quieten your mind, helps you to find that parenting instinct, to hear it and then to start to trust it. The more you spend time getting quiet and taking some time to be calm, the more you will recognise your inner voice and feel able to follow it. As you become more confident with using relaxation techniques, the more you will be able to tune into your feelings. You may find that you are able to ask your inner guide questions on tricky subjects or use this time to be able to navigate your way through issues and to make decisions.

Connection

Love is connection. Connection is love. Whether you realise it or not, connection is what your baby wants and needs and it's a basic need for you too – it is for all humans. It's hard for us to connect fully with our children when we're stressed and anxious. When we're thinking about a whole host of other things like if we're a good parent or caught up with what we think others expect from us, it makes connection difficult.

Think back to chapter two. You now know that oxytocin flows when you are calm and when you are holding your baby. You will feel that flow of oxytocin because for almost everyone it feels good. It feels like calm, like being in love and being happy. It can feel like a rush of positivity or peacefulness, you may even feel like you want to sleep. Your baby will feel all these things too, making your arms the place that they want to be. When babies are skin to skin, new neurological pathways are being formed both for babies and for parents.

Human touch, and especially that between a parent and child, increases a sense of wellbeing for all involved. It really does calm down the nervous system and help you and your baby feel calm and more content. These moments of connection build upon each other and form your relationship with your child. It's never too late to start doing them. No matter how things have been so far you can get back to connection and start building those lifelong bonds.

Guided relaxation

This isn't always easy when you have a lot of stressful things going on. Becoming a parent for the first time can feel like a big shock and very different from what you imagined. But the good thing about relaxation techniques is that the more you do them the easier they become and the more effective they are.

In a study of new mothers, it was shown that guided relaxation is the most effective form of relaxation which, in turn improves breastfeeding experiences.

Finding time can feel tricky, but it's something that is worth prioritising and making time for. If in pregnancy you can use guided relaxations, then once your baby arrives it will be something that you look forward to doing.

You can either ask a loved one to read the script to you or you can go to the resources website for a download of the MP3s that go with this book. http://mindfulbreastfeeding.co.uk/book-resources/

The Inner Garden

Find somewhere comfortable to sit or lie down. And when you are ready, gently close your eyes. Let your breathing find its natural rhythm ...... Your breath perhaps slowing now, becoming more shallow. Don't force it ...... just notice what your body is doing. Your chest, your abdomen. The feeling of the air coming into your nose or mouth ...... The sensation as it touches the back of your throat and passes down into your windpipe and lungs.

And with each breath your body becomes more relaxed ...... and if your mind wanders, if thoughts are present, simply return your attention back to your breath ......

And as you breathe and relax more, you can feel the ground or chair supporting you ...... grounding you. I would like you to visualise yourself in a beautiful woodland ...... And as you walk through the woodland you are becoming more and more relaxed ...... In front of you, you notice a stair case. It's white and you are curious to know what is at the bottom ...... As you step onto the first stair you notice it feels soft and fluffy, like feathers or like walking on clouds. Slowly you walk down the stairs, one step at a time ...... With each step you feel your body relax more and more ...... With each step you feel your muscles loosening and any tension leaving your body.

As you reach the bottom of the stairs your fingers and toes may feel tingly or your arms and legs may feel heavier or lighter. And none of this matters, they are just signs that you are feeling relaxed and calm ......

And when you reach the bottom of the stairs you see a brick wall covered in vines and little flowers. There is a little wooden door and you can't help but walk up to the door for a closer look ...... On the door is a plaque with your name on it, so you turn the handle and open the door and walk through the arch and into your garden ......

As you step though the archway, you immediately feel at ease and at peace. You know straight away that this is your garden. Your safe place. Everything here is beautiful and full of life and it's filled with flowers and plants that you love ...... Here you can be yourself ...... and as you look around your garden and take in its beauty you feel even more calm and relaxed ......

Looking around you notice an area where there are some old leaves on the ground, some twigs and autumn fall. You grab a rake and slowly start raking it all up into a pile. And as you do so you name some of the leaves and twigs with any difficult or negative feelings you have been having lately ...... They may be feelings about being pregnant, or about the birth ...... they may be thoughts about yourself, parenthood or breastfeeding. You may feel fear, anger, frustration or resentment. Just take a moment to name them ...... Now rake them up and let go of any hurtful, negative feelings or emotions ...... Once the area is cleared, if you want to, you can make a little bonfire to burn it all away ......

Taking a few more deep breaths in your special

garden. Looking around you at the beauty, feeling the peace and contentment that this place brings ......

You reach into one of your pockets and find some seeds. The seeds feel lovely to hold in your hand and as you look at them you name them. You have one for love, one for calm, one for confidence, one for forgiveness. Find a fresh patch of soil in your garden and throw them in. Water the seeds and know that they will grow, along with the rest of the beautiful flowers in your garden. And as you look, you can already see green shoots coming up ......

In your other pocket you find another, bigger seed. This one looks special, it's big and colourful. It looks like a magical seed. This seed represents your breastfeeding relationship with your new baby. Take it and hold it and tell it how you want to feel when you're holding and feeding your baby ......

And as you look around your garden again you can see the perfect place to plant this special seed. You go over there and gently place it in the earth. And as you water it, you immediately see it growing right in front of you. It's growing into the most beautiful flower you've ever seen ......

Take a few more breaths now, in your garden. Your garden of peace, a place where you feel safe and calm. As you look around, know that you can come back here at any time ......

Turning back to your breath again now. You are now going to leave your garden and go back up the stairs

...... With each step up, you are feeling a little more aware of your body and your surroundings.

1,2,3 ...feeling your body against the ground or chair.

4,5,6 ... starting to move your fingers and toes.

7, 8, 9 ... making bigger movements with your body, perhaps a stretch or a yawn.

10 ...... no rush, eyes open whenever you feel ready.

A Guided Relaxation for Parent and Baby

Find a quiet space ...... for just you and your baby. And make yourself comfortable ...... You can hold your baby on your chest, and if you want to be skin to skin with them then that may help you to relax more, but if you can't then that's OK.

Once your baby is settled, gently close your eyes ...... and take 2 or 3 deep breaths ...... That's it ......and with each breath, feel your shoulders relax more and more ...... Maybe you can breathe in your baby's beautiful scent, from the top of their head and this helps you to relax even more. And as you relax ...... feel the weight of your baby's body on your chest ...... And now bring your attention to your baby's breathing...... Noticing any little movements or noises they are making ...... Noticing the small rhythmical patterns of their breath ...... Deeper and deeper into relaxation ......

And now start to imagine a gentle warmness starting to grow inside your body ......Perhaps it has a colour or a glow ...... It's starting in the area of your heart and the same warmness and glow is starting in the heart of your baby ...... Now imagine that glow, start to flow around your body and into your lungs ...... with each breath the glow expands and starts to connect with your baby. And as you both breathe, the colour and warmth is felt by both of you.

Breathe in Love ......

Breathe out Love ......

And again. Over and over ...... Until you feel the warm glow of love and oxytocin flowing, through your body and your baby's ...... in synchronisation and almost as one ......

And as you relax here, with your baby ...... be at peace and remember that the two of you have a unique bond and connection that is not shared by anyone else in the world ...... And that whenever you want to connect with your baby at any time ...... even as they grow older, you can. You can simply recreate this relaxation and enjoy these intense feelings of love, binding attachment and well-being at any time ...... And in turn you are teaching your little one ways in which to relax and connect ......

As you open your eyes you may wish to kiss your baby's head or look into their eyes to let them know how deeply and unconditionally they are loved.

JOURNALING PROMPTS

Why not give regular relaxation time a go? Decide when you will do it and commit to 10 days. If you need to book in help with baby or other children then do it. Let those who are able to help you know that this is important to you and why.

Here is a space for you to record 10 days of relaxation practice. You may be surprised by the results. Aim for at least a 5 minute deep muscle relaxation a day and feel free to use the MP3s available to you on my website.

A 10 day relaxation journal

Here's some daily questions for you to ask yourself:

Day 1

How long did I relax for today?

Which method or guided relaxation did I use?

How easy was it to relax?

How did I feel afterwards?

Day 2

How long did I relax for today?

Which method or guided relaxation did I use?

How easy was it to relax?

How did I feel afterwards?

Day 3

How long did I relax for today?

Which method or guided relaxation did I use?

How easy was it to relax?

How did I feel afterwards?

Day 4

How long did I relax for today?

Which method or guided relaxation did I use?

How easy was it to relax?

How did I feel afterwards?

Day 5

How long did I relax for today?

Which method or guided relaxation did I use?

How easy was it to relax?

How did I feel afterwards?

Day 6

How long did I relax for today?

Which method or guided relaxation did I use?

How easy was it to relax?

How did I feel afterwards?

Day 7

How long did I relax for today?

Which method or guided relaxation did I use?

How easy was it to relax?

How did I feel afterwards?

Day 8

How long did I relax for today?

Which method or guided relaxation did I use?.

How easy was it to relax?

How did I feel afterwards?

Day 9

How long did I relax for today?

Which method or guided relaxation did I use?

How easy was it to relax?

How did I feel afterwards?

Day 10

How long did I relax for today?

Which method or guided relaxation did I use?

How easy was it to relax?

How did I feel afterwards?

chapter six
TRUST

If there is one thing that I would like you to take from reading this book it's that you start to feel more confident in listening to yourself and believing in yourself as a mother. This isn't an overnight thing, it's something that takes time and self-awareness. I talked in the last chapter about recognising and following your own inner guide. But to do this, I believe we need to have an understanding about why we don't always naturally trust our ourselves. Of course, everyone is different, as we've had different upbringings and life experiences, but generally, as women, we have not been taught to trust in ourselves, in fact we are told, almost daily, not to love who we are or what we believe in.

Ray Dodd, a Money and Business Coach, opened my eyes to this and enlightened me to the world of beauty and how products are marketed to us. Ray says:

"As women we are told our whole lives that there is something wrong with our body. Go into any beauty retail store and look at what every product is telling us. We are marketed to via our flaws and failings. Our hair may be too straight or too curly, too dry or too greasy, the wrong colour or texture. Similarly, with our skin, our body hair, our nails or teeth. Every single product is marketed to us in a way that highlights to us how imperfect out bodies are, with an undertone of what is and isn't acceptable in our society. "

Lifestyle magazines and reality TV shows, even those aimed at children and teens, increase our insecurities and advertise lifestyles and bodies that are unobtainable and actually not even real – most publications only contain airbrushed photos, anything from slimming a waist down or enhancing breasts to changing skin tones and erasing blemishes. No wonder we find it hard to feel beautiful and love our bodies just as they are. All of these feelings feed into a belief that our bodies are far from perfect and are laden with flaws.

As young girls we may have been picking up these messages from our family members too. Messages about what a beautiful body looks like or what as women we need to eat or do to look a certain way.

With these subliminal messages infiltrating our subconscious time and time again throughout our lifetime, it's hardly any wonder that when we become pregnant we have a hard time believing and trusting that our bodies can grow, birth and feed a baby.

And for expectant or new parents there is a whole new wave of being told who we should be and how we should behave. It comes from all angles: from pregnancy and parenting books, from professionals and well meaning family and friends. EVERYBODY has a view on how you should bring up your baby and to complicate matters even further all of these opinions differ and contradict each other. This can leave us feeling really confused and overwhelmed. We live in an often fear-based society and much of the advice given to new parents can feed into this, which can have the knock-on effect of making you feel anxious and again leads you away from your own intuition and trust in yourself AND in your baby.

I want to let you know that between you all as a new family – parents and baby – you have the ability to navigate your own path in parenting. Using the techniques in this book, you will find you are able to start shutting out the information from others that doesn't serve you. You will start to connect with yourself and your baby in a way that builds up your confidence and resilience as a parent. You will have the tools to be able to navigate the world of breastfeeding so that you can get the information and answers that are right for you.

Trust is pivotal to breastfeeding. Time and time again, I meet women who just don't believe in their body's ability to feed their baby. But why? You can go back to chapter one to read about all the ways that breastfeeding is undermined by commercial influences. But I ask you to think about this: When you cut your finger, do you expect it to keep bleeding? Do you worry that your platelets won't do their job and clump together to stop the bleed? Do you doubt your body's ability to heal that small cut? Unless you have a bleeding disorder the chances are that you don't give it a second thought. Yet when it comes to feeding our baby, breastfeeding so often fills us with worry or anxiety. We struggle to believe that our body can do what it is made to do. When we don't have trust in our body this distrust can in turn cause issues with breastfeeding, which can be hard to overcome without the right support. Good support doesn't undermine your instincts and fully believes that you can breastfeed your baby.

Tuning into your baby

I'm going to do a little exercise with you now. If your baby has already been born, you can still place your hands on your tummy and imagine that they are still in there.

Gently close your eyes and place your hands on your bump or where your bump would be. And just take a couple of nice deep breaths. Feel yourself becoming calmer and more relaxed.

And now I want you to tune into your baby. Imagine their life inside the womb. The noises they hear, the sensations they are experiencing. At the end of pregnancy, they are held tight in a little ball, all warm and cosy. They can hear your heartbeat, your breathing, sounds of digestion and a muffled version of your voice. The temperature for them is constant. They haven't experienced hunger, as they are continuously fed by the placenta. They are experiencing the things you eat through tasting amniotic fluid, which tastes similar to your colostrum.

Take a few more breaths now, tuning into your baby – calm and content with where they are. Knowing nothing else but what they have experienced in the womb.

When babies are born, the world can be quite a shock to them. If you can re-create what they have experienced in the womb, as closely as possible, then you make the transition from womb to world as gentle as it can be.

Babies want to be close. They want to hear the familiar sounds, the sound of your heart and your breathing. Your body can even regulate their body temperature, when they are skin to skin with you, as it reacts to their needs. Being alone in a crib or moses basket feels unfamiliar and frightening after spending nine months inside another human being. That's why babies want to be held. They are living by physiology and instincts alone. They are incapable of being sneaky, lazy, needy, greedy, difficult or any of the other labels we hear adults give to babies. They live completely in the present moment, communicating their needs to us as and when they arrive. And as new parents it's our role to meet those needs. It really is as simple as that.

Research shows that when baby's needs are met in the first year of life, that this enables optimal neurological and emotional development. We also know that when babies are held skin to skin after birth that mother's brains also develop in the way that they are supposed to, with new neural pathways being created.

The fourth trimester
Human babies are born quite helpless compared to other mammals. Most mammals are able to walk soon after birth. They can hide from predators and independently reach their mother's milk. Those who

can't walk like marsupials or primates are carried around by their mother until an age where they are able to care a little for themselves.

It can be useful to think about the first three months after your baby is born as a fourth trimester. One which is dedicated to a slow transition into the world for your little one. One where they are held close and have their needs met.

There is so much research and writing on this period of child development – far more than I'm able to go into here. But here are a couple of great books on the subject:

Mothers and Others, Sarah Blaffer Hrdy, Harvard University Press.

The Fourth Trimester, Susan Brink, University of California Press.

In our modern lives, having your baby close at all times can feel like quite a challenge. Life is just not set up for it! But in many cultures a period of "lying in" would be quite normal. Often for the first six weeks, women will be cared for by extended family whilst they focus on recovery from the birth and getting to know their baby and getting breastfeeding established. Although this may sound quite extreme to us, I think there's a lot we can learn from the concept.

Many couples will plan a Baby Moon of a week or more, where they prioritse getting to know their baby and getting breastfeeding off to a good start. A period of time with no outside demands or expectations. Of course most people want to share their new baby with others, and most families are desperate to see the new arrival. But this can quickly become a burden and something to worry about when really your mind and body are focused on the baby. In chapter seven I'll share with you some different ways to make the post-birth period work for you and your baby.

By slowing down and connecting with your baby you are starting to build a beautiful relationship with them right from the word go. You're building up a trusting relationship with them filled with love, respect and understanding.

If you're finding that connecting with your baby feels like a struggle then you may find the bonding relaxation a lovely thing to do together. Early parenting can be full of all sorts of challenges and struggles. I think it's important to know that whatever your situation, bonding with your baby doesn't always come naturally at first. It's very common for both new mums and dads to feel a certain disconnect at the start, often it's something we don't have much control over and it's not something to beat yourself up about. I urge you to share your feelings with those around you. The practices in the book can really help to start building up a stronger connection and bond with your baby.

Parenting books, websites and courses

Of which this is one! So it would be quite hypocritical of me to suggest you don't read them! However, I urge you to read all books with a questioning mind. I can't say this enough times:

every baby is an individual

every parent is an individual

We all have happy days and not so happy days. Days when we're hungry, days when we're not. Days when we want to be in stimulating environments and days when we want to be quiet and still. So I warn against any book, website or "expert" who tells you how to raise your baby, how to feed them or put them to bed on a strict schedule. These books talk as if babies are robots or in some way deviously trying to make our lives difficult. They are not. They are individual people, just like you and me. Studies show that parents who try to follow rigid routines from books are more likely to suffer from post-natal depression and when we realise that babies are as varied and individual as us, you can soon see why this is the case.

By all means take the information from books and experts that works for you. Look at research and read about normal infant development, but don't lose sight of what YOU feel is right for YOU and YOUR BABY. You actually have the answers inside of you and the more you start to trust yourself and your baby, the easier and easier it will become to shut out the should and should-nots from the outside world and do things in a way that works for you as a family.

BREAST SLEEPING

Breastfeeding and sleep

I know this is a big subject, one which is far too large to cover in depth in this book. But I have some recommendations for you below if you want to read more around this subject. When thinking about the fourth trimester, it makes complete sense that babies want to be next to us, feeling our warmth and hearing our heart beat and this is true for when they are asleep, as much as when they are awake. Up until their birth, your baby slept inside you, being jiggled around whilst being held nice and tight. If we look around at other species of mammals, it is perfectly normal for them to sleep with their young. Primates especially will have their young on their body day and night.

Research shows us that by being close by, babies use the rhythm of their parent's breathing to regulate their own and that having direct access to the breast often means a night of more sleep for both baby and mother.

However, in many Western societies, co-sleeping or bed-sharing has been frowned upon and heavily discouraged by health professionals due to perceived risks around Sudden Infant Death Syndrome (SIDS). The good news is that there is lots of evidence that suggests that it is no safer to have your baby on a separate sleeping surface. However, there is a list of risk factors, that increases the risk to your baby if you do share a sleeping surface. These are:

- Drinking Alcohol
- Smoking
- Taking drugs
- Not breastfeeding
- Using an unsafe sleeping space, such as a chair,

sofa, waterbed, or one with unsafe covers, gaps, or pillow near the baby

- An overheated baby
- A premature or low weight baby

This is one area where I strongly recommend reading the guidelines and information related to safe sleep. In the UK 50 per cent of parents will fall asleep with their baby in their bed at some point during the first three months. So it's important that everybody ensures that their bed is set up for safe bed-sharing even if you plan never to do it. Use the information available along with your instincts and what feels right for your family, to decide how sleep is going happen for you all and whatever you decide, be safely prepared to be flexible with arrangements once your baby arrives.

I recommend that babies are in their own space, next to Mum with their own blanket and lying on their back if co-sleeping is what you choose to do. If you still feel uneasy about sharing a bed with your baby, please keep in mind that sleeping with them on a chair or sofa is far more dangerous than having them in bed with you and accounts for many more Sudden Infant Deaths.

For further information, statistics and resources please go to:

https://www.basisonline.org.uk/

Books on sleep:

Sweet Sleep, La Leche League

The Gentle Sleep Book, Sarah Ockwell-Smith

Holistic Sleep Coaching, Lyndsey Hookway

Wearing your baby

As we've already established, babies like to be close. They like to be held tight and moved around, just like they were in the womb. This makes complete sense, but in reality and in our modern lives can be really challenging. This is especially true if you have a partner who has gone back to work or you have little or no help from family or a baby who really loves to be held at all times. Wearing your baby in a sling or carrier, frees up your hands and enables you to do other things whilst holding your baby at the same time. Slings and carriers can be used both out and about and around the house. If you already have other children then a sling can be an absolute life-saver, freeing you up to play and meet the needs of your other child or children.

Again the information and choices with this can feel overwhelming. In the first instance, have a look around to see if you have a local sling library. These are run by trained baby-wearing consultants, who will usually have a wide range of slings and carriers for you to look at and try on. It's fine to go in pregnancy to get an idea of what's available. You can then either try on or rent a sling before you go out and buy one. There are lots of different types, but in the early weeks a simple stretchy sling is perfect, whether it's one long piece of material that you learn to wrap yourself or one that is ready wrapped for you. It's a style that keeps your baby feeling cocooned and close to you whilst your hands are free to do the other things you want to do.

If you can't get to a sling library or baby-wearing consultant then I highly recommend doing some research online. There are safety considerations with baby-wearing and not all carriers are created equally.

To ensure your baby is safe when you're carrying them in a sling, you can keep in mind the list of TICKS.

Baby wearing TICKS:

- Tight
- In view
- Close enough to kiss
- Keep chin off chest
- Supported back

Resources:

https://www.carryingmatters.co.uk/

When parenting is all new. It can feel daunting, over-whelming and a bit of a shock. But by using the tools in this book, your confidence will start to grow and your trust in your own abilities will too. There's not really any right or wrong ways of doing this whole parenting thing. Most of us just want the best for our babies and children and will navigate our way through. Something that worked for me and my babies may not work for you. But I can share this: After 12 years of parenting, I am still winging it every single day as a mother. Some days I make good decisions and others not so good. What I've learnt over the years is that by letting go of perfectionism and what I perceive others' expectations might be, I'm able to connect to my children and husband on a deeper level, which in turn, makes navigating life's problems and dilemmas a whole lot easier.

If something particular is worrying you or is constantly on your mind, then head back to chapter four, Affirmations, and write some new positive statements around your concerns.

Searching out the answers that you need

Although we can tune into our own instincts and the needs of our baby, sometimes we need information to help us to make a decision. The problem is that in this age of information overload it's not always easy to decide which information is helpful and which isn't.

We live in fear-filled times. We have continuous access to the internet, 24-hour news channels, world events, birthing and parenting horror stories and opinions that span the whole spectrum of any subject.

Many people choose to have their babies in hospital, and westernised healthcare settings are run with safety at their forefront. This has both an upside and a downside. On the upside, birth is highly managed and therefore any potential issues picked up before they can become bigger problems. On the downside, births are highly managed which can make it hard for women to birth in their own way, causing higher rates of intervention, complex births and often birth trauma.

Hospital settings tend to follow policies and procedures. Again these have safety in mind but at the same time don't always allow for individualised care. This affects not only birth but also postnatal care. Having a list of your preferences around the first hours and days of your baby's life can really help communicate your wishes to your care givers. I highly recommend writing one. You can find a template online at:

http://mindfulbreastfeeding.co.uk/book-resources/

It can be tricky when being advised to do something by a health professional, if that advice doesn't feel quite right. Perhaps it goes against your instincts, or you worry that a course of action with feeding your baby, will affect your breastfeeding journey negatively.

When something doesn't sit quite right with you it can be useful to explore it further with your health professionals.

Sometimes it's difficult to find the words. This can be especially true when you have just had a baby. Parents are particularly vulnerable at this time. You've just experienced something pretty huge. You have a brand new little human to look after and for mothers, your hormones are changing and shifting. Go back to your feeding preference/plan to guide you. I have also listed some useful questions, that you may want to use to get the information that is helpful to you and can help you to take the course of action that feels right.

I'm struggling to breastfeed, I wonder if you can help me?

Does this look right?

Can you tell that my baby is swallowing?

Could what you're suggesting have an impact on the baby's ability to breastfeed?

Would what you're suggesting affect my ability to breastfeed?

Could you explain what that means in more detail please?

We'd like some time to think about the information you have just given us.

Is there a medical reason for what you are suggesting?

Is there any harm if we wait a while? We'd like to do that if possible.

Is the baby in danger? If not, we'd like to leave it for a little while.

What other options are there that we could consider first?

Why do you feel that this is necessary at this point?

What do you see that tells you we should do this?

Is this an emergency?

Is it likely in this case?

What will happen if we don't do this?

Are you suggesting this because it's hospital protocol or do you believe it is best for my baby? Could you tell me why?

Can you be sure that it will do more good than harm in my case? Why?

Would you put that in writing please?

If in doubt remember to think BRA

B – Benefits. What would be the benefits of doing what you suggest?

R – Risks. What might be the risks of what you are suggesting?

A – Alternatives. Are there any breastfeeding friendly alternatives?

By having the right information on hand and by knowing whether something is an emergency or not, you will feel more in control and then able to make your own informed decisions. With the right information and your instincts to guide you will start to be able to carve your own path as a parent more and more as times goes on.

JOURNALING PROMPTS

Look back at chapter three, How Breastfeeding Works. What preferences would you like to make for the first hours and days after you have given birth, to get breastfeeding off to the best start?

Below are some areas you might like to think about:

The first hour after the birth.

Your environment whilst getting to know your baby and learning to breastfeed.

Who you might ask for breastfeeding help?

What else do you need to think about or plan before breastfeeding?

For more ideas and to see the sample feeding plan, head to: http://mindfulbreastfeeding.co.uk/book-resources/

chapter seven
SUPPORT

Support comes in many forms, from our nearest and dearest to meeting new friends and finding professional support. Breastfeeding your baby is not something that you can easily do alone.

Partners

Research shows us that partners are a vital source of support for breastfeeding mothers. If you and your partner haven't started talking about breastfeeding yet, you may find it useful to look together at the journaling questions from chapters one and two.

Talking through how you both feel about breastfeeding will really help you to uncover any potential conflicts when your baby arrives.

It's important that your partner joins you for any breastfeeding education too. The more that they understand how breastfeeding works and what the early weeks might look like, the more they can plan and give the right kind of support in the early hours, days and weeks. In the journaling questions at the end of this chapter there are a few questions that you may like to think about together.

Partners can sometimes feel left out in the early weeks when there is so much feeding going on, but the truth is that there are so many other things that can be done. Here's a few of them:

- Change nappies

- Wind the baby (if needed)

- Rock and carry the baby

- Bath the baby

- Take the baby out for short walks whilst you rest

- Prepare meals

- Tidy and clean the house

- Do the food shopping

- Be the main communicator around visitors and announcements

Partners have such a varied role to play and can spend this time building up a beautiful bond with your little one in their own unique way. Bonding for the two of them is so important and with many partners returning to work in just a couple of weeks, keeping these early weeks as just your new little family can be really special and a wonderful way of settling into your new lives.

Family

Everyone will be keen to see the new baby, that goes without saying. It's such a joy to have a tiny little new member to the family. But if you have already read the earlier chapters in the book, you have probably guessed that I'm going to suggest that you think very carefully about who is around whilst you're learning to breastfeed your baby.

As I mentioned in chapter five, for breastfeeding to work you need oxytocin to flow. For oxytocin to flow, you need to be as relaxed as you can This is not always easy if you have others around. Especially if those people are not supportive of breastfeeding.

On top of this, learning to breastfeed takes time and patience. To start with it's easiest if you expose your whole breast or better still are skin to skin with your baby as much as possible. For many families this just isn't going to be easy with whole hoards of people coming to visit.

Talk it over with your partner. Use the questions at

the end of this chapter to guide you and think about how you want those early hours, days and weeks to look and then communicate this to your family and explain why.

Building your community

We really are not supposed to do this alone. You may look around you both IRL and online and see amazing mothers absolutely rocking it – make up on, hair done, skinny jeans, baby immaculately dressed with the latest buggy, meeting up with friends, looking relaxed and happy. But the truth is that life with a baby is a bit of a roller coaster. There are definitely moments when you feel on top of life and like you've got this parenting thing, but there are also many moments of feeling the opposite. I promise you that that mum who you saw was probably super stressed and having some kind of drama just hours ago!

The problem with celebrity culture, magazines and social media is that the snap shots of parenthood that we see are so often curated to capture that perfect moment. We may be completely aware of this, but when we see it all the time it starts building up a subconscious picture for us of what parenting looks like. Whether we are conscious of it or not, seeing all this stuff gives us really unrealistic expectations of parenting life.

Have a think about what you share on social media (if you do). Is it your moments of feeling low, not enough, of making mistakes or your house looking a complete tip? Generally, we don't. We want people to see the best of us, not the moments of struggle. We want to be liked and accepted, connected and often popular. So we show the side that we want others to see. But when millions of others are all doing the same, it puts across a picture of the perfect life, and before we know it it can easily become a competition in perfectionism and perfect parenting.

I'm all for keeping it real, both IRL and on social media and thankfully, there are many others that feel the same way. I'm not talking about non-stop moaning or late-night keyboard warrior rants. But I think it's important that we are honest about how we are doing. And one of the biggest parts of this is not trying to do it all, all by ourselves.

Many of those celebs you see online have masses of help behind the scenes: nannies, cooks, personal assistants and trainers. They invest in help so that they can lead the life that they want. What they understand is that they do need help. I'm a firm believer in help for mothers, of course most of us can't afford an entourage, but it doesn't mean that we need support any less.

Around the world, many people don't live in small nuclear families. Historically, women support each other, either bringing up children alongside others in their community or by having other family members living with them or close by. It's generally believed that the upbringing of a child is a group activity.

In our modern times and generally in Western society, it's not unusual to live away from our parents and extended family. In our communities, we often keep ourselves to ourselves and even if we know our neighbours, often feel uncomfortable in asking for help.

It's no surprise to me that mental health issues in the perinatal period are on the rise. When we put unrealistic expectations on ourselves and our lives at a time when we have very little help and support around in our family life, we are setting ourselves up to feel like a failure. Parenting can be a lonely business. If you have chosen to be the one on maternity leave and your partner is out at work for much of the day, then you are spending much of your day alone with a little one and having very little in the way of adult contact and conversations.

To add to this, if we are trying to show only the best of ourselves and our baby or child to others this can make meeting up with other parents really stressful. Conversations about what your baby is or isn't doing tend to feel competitive and again can lead us to feel like complete failures, but are the sorts of topics that come up again and again between new parents.

Sleep, feeding, potty training, when we talk about them with others, they can feel like measures of success – a reflection on how good a parent you are and a reflection on how "good" a baby you have. As commonplace as these conversations are, they simply lead to feelings of not being a good enough parent, of not having a good or intelligent baby, perhaps even feelings of smugness and judgement of others and their ability to parent well. Here's a simple and honest way of looking at this:

All babies are individuals with their own needs and personalities. They need love and connection, warmth and food.

It really is that simple.

Yes, we need friendships, and being with others whilst bringing up our children is a complete game-changer and I believe at the heart of happy parenting. But it only works without judgement and the need for validation, and in our modern culture this can be pretty tricky to accomplish.

Seeking out a like-minded crowd, who accepts you as you are, is trickier than it sounds, but so worth it for the connection you can feel during a time of transition and transformation – which is exactly what early parenthood is.

In a nutshell, we are all going to do this slightly differently. That the things that work for you and your baby are not necessarily going to be the right things for your sister or best friend. You may be surprised by the parenting choices made by others that you have known for a very long time, but that's OK. You can support them without judgement and without it being a reflection on you.

Finding breastfeeding support

You may need breastfeeding support and you may not, but I strongly encourage you to find your local source of breastfeeding help whilst you are pregnant.

This might be:

- A local breastfeeding group
- A breastfeeding team within your health care service
- Your local IBCLC (Certified Lactation Consultant)
- A breastfeeding volunteer helpline

A good place to start is by asking your midwife or obstetrician during one of your appointments. Ensure you ask about the training and qualifications of the person providing the support. Sadly anyone can set up a breastfeeding support service and may be providing out-of-date, incorrect or in some cases dangerous advice.

Local breastfeeding groups welcome expectant parents with open arms and will provide you with lots of information. If you visit before your baby arrives then you will know exactly where to go if you have any issues or problems once your baby is here.

When to ask for help

This may sound silly, but it's not always easy to know if and when you need help with breastfeeding. If in doubt, contact your midwife or health visitor in the first instance. If issues persist, then don't hesitate to find someone with some specialist breastfeeding training. In hospital this may be your infant feeding team, or lactation consultant. At home it might be your local breastfeeding group or IBCLC. If the support you have received hasn't helped then keep reaching out to others.

If breastfeeding is painful or if you are worried about your baby, then please don't wait, seek help straight away.

JOURNALING PROMPTS

What plans can you put in place so that breastfeeding is prioritised over the first few weeks?

How could you keep visitors down to a minimum in this time?

Who would be helpful to have around?

Who would not be helpful to be around and how will you communicate to them your wishes around them seeing you and the baby?

Who will cook and provide food for the breastfeeding parent?

Who will carry out the other household chores?

What are the things that the non-breastfeeding partner can do so that you can focus on breastfeeding?

If you are not living with a partner, who will help you and what do you need from them?

chapter eight
you

We all experience things differently as we move into a life of parenthood, but certainly for most, a whole shift in identity is happening whether you are aware of it or not. As each new child enters into the family, a huge shift occurs, and life is never exactly the same again. As parents you have a new focus and new priorities. You have the responsibility of a tiny little human being who needs you for everything. As wonderful as this can be, it can also be very challenging, especially as it's an around-the-clock role.

Having an awareness of this shift and having someone to talk to about it can really help you to navigate your feelings and emotions during this time. Perhaps you have worked full time all of your adult life and now you are going to spend a few months or even a few years away from the work place. Perhaps you will return to work as soon as possible but will now have to consider childcare and altering your work time. Maybe you were socialising in the evenings several times a week and that has started to change since being pregnant. Or you could have children already and you know that having a baby again is going to alter the time you spend with your older children as well as the entire family dynamic.

Every shift, every chapter of your life will bring with it new joys and new challenges. One of the reasons that I wrote this book was to give new parents the tools that I didn't have when my children were young. Tools that remind you to think about yourself and what you want and need, not just what the rest of your family needs.

Partners

As much as every family is different, many women still carry out many of the traditionally female roles around the house. This is despite the fact that they are more likely to be working than ever before. As well as cooking, cleaning, laundry and childcare, there are a whole host of responsibilities and things to remember that do often fall to the mother in the family. Things like arranging childcare, being the first on-call when the children are sick, remembering birthdays, buying gifts, arranging play-dates – the list goes on.

There is great news too which is that dads are now more involved with their children and with the household than ever before. More countries are giving parents equal opportunities, whatever their gender, to take leave from work when their baby comes, meaning that shared parental leave is becoming more popular. The key to making all of this work is good communication. Becoming parents is challenging and to keep your relationship healthy and strong, continuing to talk to each other about how you're feeling is vital. If this isn't something that you're very good at then I recommend seeking some help from a relationship therapist, or taking a look at courses or books on the subject. See the reference section at the back of this book.

The tools in this book can work for both of you so don't be afraid to share them with your partner. I have so many lovely testimonials from Mindful Breastfeeding Practitioners who have finished breastfeeding support visits by reading a guided relaxation to the whole family – leaving them in a bubble of oxytocin. Give it a go. It really does work! If you are parenting alongside another and you're finding things tough, then it's likely that they are too. Find time to talk and be honest about how your feeling and listen fully to your partner too.

Below I talk about finding time for some self-care, but I also think it's important to take some moments of time with your partner. It's easy to get caught up with nappies, feeds and snatching a moment to eat some food – hands free. Often the couples I work with are sleeping separately in the early weeks and sometimes for months, so remembering to make physical contact with each other at times throughout the day is important – even just some eye contact, a touch on the knee or a quick hug can help you feel more connected during what can be an exhausting time. As your baby gets older you'll find it easier to do things together, like watching a whole movie or going out on a date. Once you're parents, these things take a little bit of planning, but it's definitely worth the effort.

Single parents

If you are parenting alone then it's vital that you find someone to talk to as well. The shift in identity that occurs around this time can leave you feeling quite at sea. I think this is partly because being a parent is almost always different to what we imagined. Prioritise finding a local baby group or class that you can go to, so that you can chat to other parents and if you have close family members or friends who are offering help or company then take them up on it.

Time

One of the biggest surprises when a baby comes along is how little time you have to yourself. Sometimes it can be hard to remember quite what you used to fill your spare time with! Some people find that they feel resentment towards their baby because their life has changed so much, and they don't have time for their own interests and needs anymore. For many, the relentlessness of having a baby on their body for much of the day and night can feel suffocating at times. All of these feelings are completely natural and normal and they're likely to fluctuate from one day to the next.

Talking these feelings through can really help, whether it's with family, friends or a professional, it's important that you share when you're finding things tough.

Self-care is one of the key concepts of Mindful Breastfeeding. Mindful Breastfeeding encourages you to be aware of how you're feeling and gives you simple tools to help you relax and feel calmer. By giving yourself a little bit of time for yourself, each day if possible, you will start to feel the benefits. When you're caring for a baby or child it's very hard to put yourself first, even for a minute. Even going to the toilet alone is almost impossible in the early years, let alone having a peaceful shower. So, as silly as it sounds, I recommend booking in some time for yourself each day as a priority. Whether it's 5 minutes, 30 minutes or an hour, book the time in with your partner or someone else who can be with the baby, so that you can have some uninterrupted space. Prioritise it and let others know why it's important to you.

Using the Mindful Breastfeeding tools

By giving yourself 15 minutes a day to first check in with how you're feeling and then focus on relaxing your body and your mind, you're likely to start feeling calmer and more in control. You'll also feel more resilient and have more energy when you're having time with you baby. Here are some ideas from this book that you can use for any moments of space and time you have to yourself.

- Journal on how you're feeling and /or how you want to feel

- Write an affirmation about something you're struggling with

- Spend 5 minutes breathing deeply

- Listen to a guided meditation

- Put on some relaxing music and close your eyes

- Sit quietly with some essential oils in a diffuser

Of course you don't have to do the above if you find you have some time to yourself. What else do you enjoy doing? Walking the dog? Having a bath? A phone call with a friend? Having your hair cut? Make time to do these things for yourself. And don't be afraid to ask for help for these things too. You deserve it, and prioritising self-care can help you to be a calmer and more connected parent.

Self-care with your baby

Finding the time or the help to practise self-care is not always possible, so it's essential that you find enjoyable, relaxing and cup-filling activities that you can do with your little one or little ones in tow. In the journaling prompts there are some questions to get you thinking about what exactly it is that you like to do and then think about how you can adapt these to the time and situations you have available.

Think about what relaxes you and what energises you. What is it about these activities that you love? If you love being at the beach because you love the sounds of the waves and fresh air – prioritise getting outside with your baby and going for a walk, perhaps somewhere near water.

If you love a long soak in a tub filled with bubble bath but know you won't be able to do that today as your baby wants to be close, then perhaps you could light a candle or put your favourite essential oil in a diffuser. Pop your favourite relaxing music on and it may feel like you're treating yourself. Maybe you could even manage a relaxing bath with your baby.

If you spend some time each day thinking about what it is you need not just what your baby needs and plan some according activities, then you are less likely to feel overwhelmed and resentful. It's so essential that we are kind and loving to ourselves and not just to others. We spend so much time celebrating new babies but we mustn't forget new mothers. The more that you can meet your own needs, the happier and more able you will be to meet the needs of your family. It's a great habit for life and especially for parenthood.

JOURNALING PROMPTS

What is your favourite thing to do? Something that makes you happy and relaxed.

Choose 3 aspects of this activity that make it feel so great. Why do you love doing the above?

List other ways that you could enjoy those aspects in your life:

If you had 3 hours

If you had half an hour

With your baby

As we come to the end of the book, I really hope that you feel more confident and knowledgeable about feeding your baby. I hope that the tools I have shared have helped you to think about what's important to you and what choices you may like to make going forwards. Do dip back into the book as and when you need to. Repeat the journaling questions. You may be surprised at what comes up! You may also find it useful to return to some of the chapters as you start breastfeeding, so pop this book into your hospital bag or on your bedside table so that you have the information, pictures and resources at hand.

One thing I can promise you along this journey is that there will be ups and downs, beautiful moments of pure joy and some very tough ones too. Parenting can be messy, confusing and fun. Every stage holds new surprises. But in amongst all of that I wish for you calm moments and connection as a family. Be kind to yourself. Be proud of the little things you achieve. Enjoy getting to know your new baby and don't be afraid to reach out for help if you're struggling in any way.

Thank you

I have so many people to thank for this book.

I have to start with the breastfeeding families that I have worked with, and especially those who have embraced the Mindful Breastfeeding tools. You inspire me with your honesty, dedication and openness to trying out something new.

Ray Dodd, who created the Mindful Breastfeeding concept with me and who continues to support and encourage me to take it to as many families and professionals as possible. To my mentor Suzy Ashworth who has believed in me from the moment we met and was a sounding board for my fears and doubts. Saveria Upcraft who coached me through the book writing process, encouraging me to keep going at each stage.

Jemma, it has been such a pleasure working with you on this project. Your illustrations and understanding of the concept of the book have been spot on and I can't wait to get started on book 2 with you! To my Mum, Pat Saunders, who had the arduous task of editing my first book and for giving me her honest feedback and suggestions. As well as helping out with childcare whenever it's needed.

To everyone who has trained with me in Mindful Breastfeeding techniques over the last few years and who has believed in the concept and the real difference it can make to new families – sharing your happy stories with me along the way. With a special mention of Laura Berkeley and Sian Aldis, who have not only entirely embraced this way of providing breastfeeding support, but keep me going through their enthusiasm and support of the work I do. Really ladies, it means the world to me, thank you so much!

To my amazing husband Paul, who is here by my side, day in and day out, navigating the complexities of parenthood and following our own dreams too. Thank you for holding the fort whilst I help other families. And to my Dad who will always entertain the kids whilst I get a teenie bit more work done. We all appreciate it.

Finally to you. For your interest in my book and Mindful Breastfeeding itself. I really do appreciate your investment and I hope that you got something from reading it – helping you on your parenting journey and your relationship with your little one.

Resources

Anna's Online Course

The Mindful Breastfeeding School.
www.themindfulbreastfeedingschool.com

Books about breastfeeding

The Womanly Art of Breastfeeding (8th Ed), La Leche League

The Positive Breastfeeding Book, Amy Brown

The Baby Feeding Book, Vanessa Christie

You've Got it in You: A Positive Guide to Breastfeeding, Emma Pickett

Mothers and Others, Sarah Blaffer Hrdy.

The Forth Trimester, Susan Brink

Making More milk, Diana West

The first forty days, Heng Ou

Books on sleep

Sweet Sleep, La Leche League

The Gentle Sleep Book, Sarah Ockwell-Smith

Holistic Sleep Coaching, Lyndsey Hookway

Books on mental wellbeing and mindfulness

Happy, Ferne Cotton

Mindfulness, Mark Williams and Penman

Mental Health online resources

Mind:
https://www.mind.org.uk/information-support/

Pandas Foundation:
http://www.pandasfoundation.org.uk/

Family Action:
https://www.family-action.org.uk/what-we-do/early-years/perinatal-support-services/

Breastfeeding Websites

Le Leche league:
https://www.laleche.org.uk/get-support/

The National Breastfeeding Helpline:
https://www.nationalbreastfeedinghelpline.org.uk/

Association of Breastfeeding Mothers:
https://abm.me.uk/get-breastfeeding-support/

Breastfeeding information:
www.breastfeeding.support

National Childbirth Trust (NCT) Helpline:
0300 330 0700

Find an IBCLC UK:
https://www.lcgb.org/find-an-ibclc/

Le Leche League: https://www.llli.org/get-help/

Lamaze: https://www.lamaze.org/nursing-resources

Basis online: (sleep information)

Bibliography

Chapter One: Understanding Infant Feeding

Amy Brown (2016) *Breastfeeding Uncovered*. Pinter and Martin

Carnegie Museum of Natural History (2011) Discovery of a 160-million-year-old fossil represents a new milestone in early mammal evolution. *Nature Journal*, 24/8/11

https://www.worldbreastfeedingtrends.org/

https://www.gov.uk/government/collections/breastfeeding-statistics

Tigers (2014) Danis Tanoik. Sikhya Entertainment and ASAP Films

Chapter Two: Your Brain

Carlson, L.E., Beattie, T.L. Giese-Davis, J., Faris, P., Tamagawa, R., Fick, L.J., Degelman, E.S. & Speca, M. (2014). Mindfulness-based cancer recovery and supportive-expressive therapy maintain telomere length relative to controls in distressed breast cancer survivors. *Cancer, 2015Feb1: 121(3): 476–484*. DOI: 10.1002/cncr.29063

Feher, S.D.K., Berger, L.R., Johnson, J.D., Wilde, J.B. (1989) Increasing Breast Milk Production for Premature Infants With a Relaxation/Imagery

Audiotape. *Pediatrics.* 1989;83(1):57–60

Kerstin, Uvnäs Moberg (2003) *The Oxytocin Factor.* Pinter and Martin

McCorry, L. K. (2007). Physiology of the autonomic nervous system. *American journal of pharmaceutical education, 71*(4), 78. doi:10.5688/aj710478

Newton, Michael et al (1958) The Effect of Intranasal Administration of Oxytocin on the Let-Down of Milk in Lactating Women. *American Journal of Obstetrics & Gynecology, Volume 76, Issue 1, 103–107*

Wu, T., Kansaku, K. & Hallett, M. (2004) How Self-Initiated Memorized Movements Become Automatic: A Functional MRI Study. *J. Neurophysiol.* 91, 1690

Chapter Three: How Breastfeeding Works

Ballard, O., & Morrow, A.L. (2013). Human milk composition: nutrients and bioactive factors. *Pediatric clinics of North America, 60*(1), 49–74. doi:10.1016/j.pcl.2012.10.002

Crenshaw J.T. (2014). Healthy Birth Practice #6: Keep Mother and Baby Together- It's Best for Mother, Baby, and Breastfeeding. *The Journal of Perinatal Education, 23*(4), 211–217. doi:10.1891/1058–1243.23.4.211

Esteves, T.M., Daumas, R.P., Oliveira, M.I., Andrade, C.A., & Leite, I.C. (2014) Factors associated to breastfeeding in the first hour of life: systematic review. *Revista de saude publica*, *48*(4), 697–708. doi:10.1590/s0034-8910.2014048005278

Geddes, D.T. (2007) Inside the lactating breast: The latest anatomy research. *J Midwifery Womens Health*. Nov-Dec;52(6):556–63

Riordan, J. & Wambach, K. (2015) *Breastfeeding and Human Lactation*, Enhanced Fifth Edition. Jones and Bartlett Publishers

Xiaoli Huang, Liling Chen, Li Zhang (2019) Effects of Paternal Skin-to-Skin Contact in Newborns and Fathers After Cesarean Delivery. *Journal of Perinatal & Neonatal Nursing, 33 (1): 68–73*

Chapter Four: Positive Self-talk

Cascio, C.N., O'donnell, M.B., Tinney, F J., Lieberman, M.D., Taylor, S.E., Strecher, V.J., & Falk, E.B. (2015). Self-affirmation activates brain systems associated with self-related processing and reward and is reinforced by future orientation. *Social Cognitive and Affective Neuroscience, 11*(4), 621–629.

Cohen, G.L., & Sherman, D.K. (2014). The psychology of change: Self-affirmation and social psychological intervention. *Annual Review of Psychology, 65*, 333–371

Gustavson, D.E., du Pont, A., Whisman, M.A., & Miyake, A. (2018). Evidence for Transdiagnostic Repetitive Negative Thinking and Its Association with Rumination, Worry, and Depression and Anxiety

Symptoms: A Commonality Analysis. *Collabra. Psychology, 4* (1), 13. doi:10.1525/collabra.128

O'Brien M., Buikstra E. & Hegney D. (2008) The influence of psychological factors on breastfeeding duration. *Journal of Advanced Nursing* 63(4), 397–408

Chapter Five: Relaxation

Feher S.D.K., Berger L.R., Johnson J.D., Wilde J.B. (1989) Increasing Breast Milk Production for Premature Infants With a Relaxation/Imagery Audiotape. Pediatrics. 83(1):57–60

Hauck, Y.L., Summers, L., White, E. *et al.* A qualitative study of Western Australian women's perceptions of using a Snoezelen room for breastfeeding during their postpartum hospital stay. *Int Breastfeed J* 3, 20 (2008) doi:10.1186/1746-4358-3-20

Keith D.R., Weaver, B.S., Vogel R.L. (2012) The Effect of Music-Based Listening Interventions on the Volume, Fat Content, and Caloric Content of Breast Milk Produced by Mothers of Premature and Critically Ill Infants. *Adv Neonatal Care.* 12(2): 112–9. 14

Nurul Husna Mohd Shukri, Jonathan Wells, Simon Eaton, Firdaus Mukhtar, Ana Petelin, Zala Jenko-Pražnikar, Mary Fewtrell (2019) Randomized controlled trial investigating the effects of a breastfeeding relaxation intervention on maternal psychological state, breast milk outcomes, and infant behavior and growth, *The American Journal of Clinical Nutrition*, Volume 110, Issue 1, July, 121–130,

Stube A., Grewen K., Pedersen C., Propper C., Meltzer-Brody S. (2012) Failed Lactation and Perinatal Depression: Common Problems with Shared Neuroendocrine Mechanisms. *Journal of Woman's Health* Vol 21, number 3

Chapter Six: Trust

www.basisonline.org.uk

Esposito G., Yoshida S., Ohnishi R., Tsuneoka Y., Rostagno Mdel C., Yokota S., Okabe S., Kamiya K., Hoshino M., Shimizu M., Venuti P., Kikusui T., Kato T., Kuroda K.O. (2013) Infant calming responses during maternal carrying in humans and mice. May 6;23(9):739-45. doi: 10.1016/j.cub.2013.03.041. Epub 2013 Apr 18

Winston, R., & Chicot, R. (2016) The importance of early bonding on the long-term mental health and resilience of children. *London journal of primary care*, *8*(1), 12–14. doi:10.1080/17571472.2015.1133012

Chapter Seven: Support

Lawrence R.A. (2002) Peer support: making a difference in breast-feeding duration. *CMAJ : Canadian Medical Association journal = journal de l'Association medicale canadienne, 166*(1), 42–43.

Tohotoa, J., Maycock, B., Hauck, Y.L., Howat, P., Burns, S., & Binns, C.W. (2009) Dads make a difference: an exploratory study of paternal support for breastfeeding in Perth, Western Australia. *International breastfeeding journal, 4,* 15. doi:10.1186/1746-4358-4-15

Sarah Blaffer Hrdy (2011) *Mothers and Others.* Harvard University Press

Chapter Eight: You

Office for national statistics (2015) changes in the value and division of unpaid care work in the uk 2000 to 2015

Harrington B., Sabatini Fraone J. (2017) *The New Dad The career-caregiving conflict.* Boston College

About the Author

Anna Le Grange is a Registered Paediatric Nurse, International Board Certified Lactation Consultant (IBCLC) and Mindfulness Coach. She has worked with new families for over 20 years as a nanny and nurse, both on hospital wards and in the community. Anna has specialised in  breastfeeding support and education since 2012.

In 2017 Anna founded The Mindful Breastfeeding School, so that she could share how Mindfulness-based breastfeeding support could help families have a more positive and fulfilling breastfeeding experience. As well as working one to one with families, Anna teaches Mindful Breastfeeding techniques to professionals both in the UK and abroad. She regularly speaks and writes about the mind-body connection and how it can make all the difference when supporting families.

Anna Lives in Kent, UK with her husband and 3 children.

Made in the USA
Coppell, TX
15 August 2021

60527121R00085